Cambridge Elements ≡

Elements in the Politics of Development
edited by
Melani Cammett
Harvard University
Rachel Beatty Riedl
Einaudi Center for International Studies and Cornell University
Ben Ross Schneider
Massachusetts Institute of Technology

Mario Einaudi
CENTER FOR
INTERNATIONAL STUDIES

 MIT CENTER FOR INTERNATIONAL STUDIES

EVERYDAY CHOICES

The Role of Competing Authorities and Social Institutions in Politics and Development

Ellen M. Lust
University of Gothenburg

CAMBRIDGE
UNIVERSITY PRESS

Shaftesbury Road, Cambridge CB2 8EA, United Kingdom

One Liberty Plaza, 20th Floor, New York, NY 10006, USA

477 Williamstown Road, Port Melbourne, VIC 3207, Australia

314–321, 3rd Floor, Plot 3, Splendor Forum, Jasola District Centre,
New Delhi – 110025, India

103 Penang Road, #05–06/07, Visioncrest Commercial, Singapore 238467

Cambridge University Press is part of Cambridge University Press & Assessment,
a department of the University of Cambridge.

We share the University's mission to contribute to society through the pursuit of
education, learning and research at the highest international levels of excellence.

www.cambridge.org
Information on this title: www.cambridge.org/9781009306126

DOI: 10.1017/9781009306164

When citing this work, please include a reference to the DOI 10.1017/9781009306164

First published 2022

A catalogue record for this publication is available from the British Library.

ISBN 978-1-009-30612-6 Paperback
ISSN 2515-1584 (online)
ISSN 2515-1576 (print)

Additional resources for this publication at www.cambridge.org/everydaychoices.

Everyday Choices

The Role of Competing Authorities and Social Institutions in Politics and Development

Elements in the Politics of Development

DOI: 10.1017/9781009306164
First published online: November 2022

Ellen M. Lust
University of Gothenburg
Author for correspondence: Ellen M. Lust, ellen.lust@gu.se

Abstract: Scholars and practitioners seek development solutions through the engineering and strengthening of state institutions. Yet, the state is not the only or often even the primary arena shaping how citizens, service providers, and state officials engage in actions that constitute politics and development. These individuals are members of religious orders, ethnic communities, and other groups that make claims on them, creating incentives that shape their actions. Recognizing how individuals experience these claims and view the choices before them is essential to understanding political processes and development outcomes. Taking an institutional approach, this Element explains how the salience of arenas of authority associated with various communities and the nature of social institutions within them affect politics and development. It establishes a framework of politics and development that allows for knowledge accumulation, guides future research, and can facilitate effective programming. This title is also available as Open Access on Cambridge Core.

This Element also has a video abstract: www.cambridge.org/ellenmlust

Keywords: development, social institutions, political behaviour, authority, service provision

ISBNs: 9781009306126 (PB), 9781009306164 (OC)
ISSNs: 2515-1584 (online), 2515-1576 (print)

Contents

A further Online Appendix can be accessed at
www.cambridge.org/everydaychoices

1 Introduction

Conventional, state-centric approaches to politics and development often cannot explain political behaviour and development outcomes. Consider the following: a Ghanaian bureaucrat, learning that her chief has entered the queue for service, draws him to the front of the line and proceeds to process his papers. A Yemeni policeman, intent on arresting a citizen for a criminal offence, seeks permission from a local shaykh before making the arrest. A Jordanian voter supports a candidate from her tribe, even though she neither likes the candidate nor expects him to win. An American in South Dakota heeds a bishop's call to be vaccinated, but he would not listen to the same call if it was made by either his senator or the head of his state's medical association.

At first glance, these are prime examples of corruption, inefficiency, and irrationality. The Ghanaian bureaucrat has violated administrative rules that prescribe equal treatment to citizens, regardless of identity. The Yemeni police-man has wasted precious time and effort to approach the shaykh, whose permission is not technically required, before making the arrest. The Jordanian voted neither in her interest nor strategically, casting a ballot for someone she neither likes nor expects to win. And the American listened to his religious leader rather than the politician, who presumably best understands the necessary policy measures, or the physician, who has medical expertise.

Such choices are not only common but also demonstrate rational compliance with institutional rules. They are explained by the fact that citizens, public service providers, and even state officials are members of various communities – such as religious orders, family or kinship groups, or ethnic communities – which make claims on them and shape their actions. The Ghanaian bureaucrat is also a tribal member, expected to show deference to her chief. She realizes that failing to do so is both disrespectful and undermines relationships with her tribal community, which often forms the 'de facto insurance model [for] millions of Africans' (Pankani, 2014, p. 26). The Yemeni policeman, embedded in a tribal system, recognizes that shaykhs view arrests of 'their' tribal members as a threat to their sovereignty and an affront to their honour. The officer knows that it 'would be a foolhardy official who imprisoned a man without his shaykh's permission', and thus allows the shaykh to deliver suspects into government custody in order to avoid confrontation (Weir, 2007, p. 188). The Jordanian voter sees casting her ballot as a chance to demonstrate allegiance to her kin and help to demonstrate their 'presence' on a national stage, as much as a chance to choose a Member of Parliament (Lust-Okar, 2009). And the South Dakotan needs to respect the religious leader, whose authority and influence extend far beyond spiritual matters (Viskupic and Wiltse, 2022). The political capture, corruption, and clientelism that frustrate analysts and policymakers are often better understood as the 'winning out' of, and compliance with, social institutions in competing arenas of authority.

Indeed, acts frequently understood solely as political behaviour or public service provision, associated with the state, are often also social acts. Those attending to a patient at a public clinic, upholding public order, or engaging in elections are likewise members of religious, geographic, kinship, and other communities, associated with arenas of authority and attendant social institutions. These social institutions dictate the roles individuals hold, shape the distribution of power, delineate acceptable behaviour, and determine the benefits of compliance and the costs of transgression. They also affect how people make sense of the world. This gives behaviours new meanings, or what Lisa Wedeen (2002) calls 'multiple significations'. Public service delivery and political engagement are not only a chance to heal the sick, maintain security, or select an official representative, but they are also often opportunities to respond to social obligations, maintain networks that provide social assistance, demonstrate respect for elders, and safeguard social order.

Thus, the state and its institutions are not the only, or even always the most important, drivers of the everyday choices that constitute politics and development. The functions typically associated with the state (e.g., the exercise of power leading to the provision of services, security, and community welfare) are in fact not *state* imperatives but essentials for any organized community. Moreover, individuals who engage in these efforts are not only citizens but also members of other communities. As such, they have a shared identity and an interest in enhancing the community welfare and perpetuating its existence. They exist within *arenas of authority* – spheres of engagement that are characterized by expected allegiances, established authorities, and distributions of power. And within these arenas, individuals' actions are shaped by *social institutions*, which seek to circumscribe the individuals' actions over sets of issues in an attempt to ensure the community's survival. These define roles within the community, the rules of engagement, and rewards that result.

The insight that actors and institutions outside the state affect political actions is not new. As early as the 1970s, Peter Ekeh (1975) argued that Africa had two 'publics': a 'primordial public', in which 'primordial groupings, ties, and sentiments influence and determine the individual's public behaviour', and a 'civic public', which was 'historically associated with the colonial administration'. James Scott (1972), writing at nearly the same time, turned our attention to how patron–client relationships – or the social 'exchange relationships between roles' – affected elections and parties. Yet, these analysts and others that followed them privileged the state as they sought to understand politics and craft development programmes.[1] They viewed an effective state as the sine qua non of good governance and development, and placed social – or 'non-state' – actors and institutions in juxtaposition to it: they simply reinforce, complement, or replace state institutions. Indeed, the very existence of influential authorities and institutions outside the state can be evidence of pathology. In the conventional view of an ideal world, non-state authorities and social institutions are not the primary drivers of appropriate political behaviour and development.

1.1 Privileging the State

That conventional approaches to politics and development privilege the state is perhaps not surprising. The scholars, practitioners, and policymakers aiming to shape the distribution of power and resources in a manner that enhances human welfare – that is, to engage in the essence of politics and development – are closely linked to the state. They often sit in or hail from departments of government, politics, or economics, where – at least since Gerschenkron (1952) – the state is considered to be the driving force behind development. They work with or in the World Bank, the United Nations Development Program, and other multilateral organizations, for whom states are both the major funders and primary interlocutors. They use available official (i.e., state-based) statistics, gathered by the state's machinery in the interest of legibility, to implement research, pinpoint citizens' needs, and assess policy impacts.

These scholars, practitioners, and policymakers generally focus on the strength of the state or the nature of its institutions, and they seek development solutions through state-building or institutional engineering. Even when they take social and economic contexts into account, considering how social identities or endowments affect outcomes, they largely overlook the variation in social institutions that compete or intersect with political institutions to shape individuals' actions. In the state-centric perspective, outcomes that deviate from expectations are 'failures': problems of 'corruption' or 'clientelism' to be solved through the strengthening and reform of state institutions.

The dominant state-centric perspective impedes our efforts to bring non-state arenas of authority and social institutions fully into the study of, and programming around, politics and development. First, it portrays actors and institutions as *either* state *or* non-state, ignoring differences among non-state arenas and institutions. Empirically there are multiple arenas outside the state, based on different notions of community (i.e., religion, ethnicity, locality, economy),

---

[1] Both Scott (1972, p. 91) and Ekeh (1975, p. 92) explicitly view clientelism and primordial publics as something to be outgrown over time.

with different distributions of power and institutional arrangements. Yet, scholars, practitioners, and policymakers too frequently lump these together as an undifferentiated 'residual', focusing on the absence of 'healthy' state institutions rather than the presence of alternatives that drive outcomes. Other times, they focus on a single arena – for instance, the relationship between tribe and state, religion and politics, or ethnicity and service provision. In doing so, they often overlook important questions about the extent to which different arenas and institutions drive development.

Second, the focus on the state diverts the efforts of political scientists and development specialists away from developing a comprehensive and coherent framework for understanding non-state arenas of authority and related social institutions. Contrast the conceptualization and study of the state and its institutions with that of other arenas of authority and associated social institutions. Particularly since Skocpol (1985) called on scholars to 'Bring the State Back In' and March and Olsen (1984) (re)turned our attention to institutions, the state and its institutions have been a centre of attention. It is an entity with notions of communities and belonging (nations), regimes and authority, which shape the distribution of power and constrain members in ways that go beyond the sum of its institutions. The state is also recognized as having independent interests and more or less autonomy from societal actors (i.e., strength). Moreover, its institutions are distinguished in terms of (relatively) well-developed conceptual categories (e.g., democracies and autocracies, centralized and decentralized administration, proportional representation or majoritarian electoral systems). Explicitly recognizing variations in state strength and institutional arrangements facilitates theory testing, helps clarify scope conditions within which theories should hold, allows for distinguishing between institutional and contextual factors, and provides a scaffolding on which to place new findings.

The study of non-state arenas and social institutions lacks such crisp, well-established conceptual categories and frameworks of study. Political scientists recognize arenas of authority outside the state and related social institutions, but the language and frameworks they employ are less fully elaborated than those used to study the state's role in governance and development. Researchers and practitioners recognize the importance of different non-state authorities, but they often focus on specific authorities (e.g., traditional authorities, gang leaders, warlords) and thus leave open questions of when and why different authorities have influence.[2] So too, they use the term 'social institutions' to denote very different concepts, ranging from *organizations*

---

[2] On different forms of non-state authorities, see Arjona (2016), Arjona et al. (2015), Baldwin (2016), Cammett and MacLean (2014), Cruz et al. (2020), Magaloni et al. (2020), Murtazashvili (2016), and Post et al. (2017).

that are either non- or semi-state[3] to informal rules followed by state actors (e.g., Helmke and Levitsky, 2004; 2006). Finally, researchers highlight different aspects of non-state arenas and social institutions, focusing on networks or specific rules.[4] However, they do not place these components in a broader framework. Without a unified language and framework of study, it is difficult to compare or reconcile diverse findings, accumulate knowledge, and achieve theoretical advances and practical insights for programming.

Third, and somewhat ironically, a state-centric approach impedes the study of the state. Assuming state predominance and under-theorizing social institutions not only precludes a full understanding of how social authorities and institutions affect governance and development outcomes, but it also distorts the view of the state. Reducing social institutions to context and under-specifying their variation makes it difficult to understand the role that state institutions truly play. Where the state is weak and social authorities are readily visible, their presence is viewed as a problem to be solved rather than forces to be understood. Where the state is apparently strong, social authorities and institutions are viewed as ineffectual and unimportant, even though they may be critical in shaping governance. Even multi- and bilateral development agents for whom state actors will remain the primary interlocutors need a clearer understanding of non-state arenas of authority and social institutions in order to be effective.

1.2 Competing Claims and Individuals' Choices

The perspective I present here is not simply that non-state arenas of authority and associated social institutions shape individuals' choices but that multiple communities often vie for control over their actions. The Ghanaian bureaucrat, Yemeni policeman, Jordanian voter, and American citizen presented earlier do not respond *only* to their kin, tribe, or religious arenas of authority any more than they respond solely to the state. The strengths of arenas vary across space and time, as well as for different individuals, depending on their position within the community (e.g., leader versus follower, elder versus youth). Often, the inelasticity of social demands becomes all too evident; particularly within development settings, institutions outside the state that shape actions lead to outcomes contra state and programming objectives. At other times, the state

---

[3] These include, for instance, unelected, non-state local governance councils analysed by Khan Mohmand and Mihajlović (2016) or service-providing organizations that are the focus of Cammett and MacLean (2014).

[4] On networks, see Arias et al. (2019), Cruz (2019), Cruz et al. (2020), and Ravanilla et al. (2021). Rules include those regarding altruism, reciprocity, or group boundary maintenance (Ambec, 2008; Bowles et al., 2003; Fearon and Laitin, 1996; Kruks-Wisner, 2018; Lieberman, 2009) and lineage systems (Brulé and Gaikwad, 2021; Robinson and Gottlieb, 2019).

may wrest control from even powerful non-state authorities, either by acting alone or in conjunction with other arenas.

The social institutions within arenas of authority also vary, creating different incentives for members within them. Expectations differ across even seemingly identical arenas of authority. Take, for example, local and international religious arenas – even of the same denomination. At times, these make competing demands on members, forcing members to choose between them. This was evident over the backlash to Pope Francis' 2016 *Amoris Laetitia*. Papal supremacy called for holistic sexual education for children, reintegration of divorced and remarried Catholics into the church, and respect for LGBTQ individuals, but many local dioceses – and a great number of individual Catholics – chose to ignore this newest apostolic exhortation. Therefore, in voting for the 'bathroom bills', proposed in US state legislatures between 2017 and 2019 as a way to limit accommodation of non-cisgender individuals, the arena of authority governing Catholic voters' decisions could be *either* aligned with the Papal seat (which would be against the restrictive legislation) *or* with the competing religious interpretation within their local community (thereby validating discriminatory practices against LGBTQ individuals). When multiple arenas of authority make contradictory demands, individuals are forced to respond to some arenas over others.

Thus, understanding political behaviour and development outcomes requires that one recognizes both the importance of competing arenas of authority and the nature of the social institutions within them. Rather than view citizens and state officials as relating their actions solely, or even primarily, to the state, I argue that we need to start by considering how individuals – voters, public service providers, bureaucrats, politicians, and others – understand the acts in which they engage. Actions such as voting, dispute resolution, and public service provision *are engagements with the state, but they are also, critically, engagements in multiple other arenas of authority.* So too, actors are not 'either' state or non-state, political or social, but often acting simultaneously as players in multiple arenas. The apt question is not 'is the service provision, election, or political behaviour in question located within the state realm?' – and thus shaped by state institutions – but rather, 'when individuals engage in these actions, what meaning do they attach to the actions?' Which arenas of authority make demands upon them, what do they believe is expected of them in each, and with what consequences?

1.3 Plan of the Element

In this Element, I aim to overcome problems of the dominant state-centric perspective by setting state and non-state authorities and institutions on equal intellectual footing, providing a structure for accumulating knowledge about how these competing arenas and social institutions influence politics and development, and reconsidering the state. To do so, I take a 'bottom-up' approach that focuses on the perspective of individuals – voters, public service providers, bureaucrats, politicians, and others – and considers how their simultaneous membership in various arenas of authority shapes their choices and, ultimately, governance and development. I focus on how the everyday choices before individuals may take multiple meanings, provide guidance on how to understand the extent to which different arenas of authority influence actions, and illustrate how differences in social institutions affect individual choices and outcomes.

This Element is intended for two audiences. For scholars, I aim to bring together currently disparate findings from extant research, highlight general themes found in empirically rich but contextually specific (and less accessible) regional studies, provide a new perspective on governance and development, and pose questions for future research. For practitioners, I hope to help develop a structure for programming that is less prone to problems of isomorphism and state centricity than conventional approaches, and yet also less indeterminant than some of the existing alternative approaches. The goal is to provide a structure and language that allow scholars, practitioners, and others interested in politics and development to make sense of the many compelling studies to date, to structure research moving forward, and to design programmes that take these findings into account.

The Element proceeds as follows. Section 2 reviews the literature. It finds that state-centric and institutional approaches have dominated the study of and programming around political behaviour and development, while alternative approaches that highlight the complexity of development make it difficult for scholars and programmers to build on past experiences. Section 3 presents arenas of authority and social institutions, the building blocks of the framework. Sections 4–6 examine how arenas of authority and the social institutions within them affect political behaviour and development. Section 4 provides guidance on how to determine the extent to which competing arenas of authority influence decisions at the core of politics and development, while Section 5 turns attention to how variations in the social institutions within these arenas shape outcomes. Section 6 examines how social institutions within the arenas of authority outside the state affect state institutions. Section 7 concludes by considering how we can use the approach presented here in future research and programming and exploring unanswered questions.

Before proceeding, two caveats are in order. First, although I adopt the language of state and non-state institutions, I am uneasy with the distinction.

As argued in Section 6, the distinction between state and non-state institutions is often overdrawn, and the boundary itself may be a useful subject of enquiry (see Mitchell, 1991). It is perhaps more apt to speak in terms of the basis of authority on which actors and institutions rest. The second caveat relates to the scope of this Element. I focus on the Global South throughout much of this text, but the social institutions discussed are not limited to what Western readers may think of as 'those places'. I emphasize the Global South because that is where the vast majority of programming is implemented, but the issues raised very much describe life in Gothenburg, Sweden; New Haven, Connecticut; Marshall, Michigan; and elsewhere as well.

2 State Centrality in Politics and Development

This section examines how the existing literature on politics and development addresses arenas of authority outside the state and the social institutions within them. Broadly speaking, there are four approaches. I call the first two 'conventional approaches'. Both place the state and its institutions centre stage and presume a duality between state and society. The first approach focuses directly on the state, while the second emphasizes society. A third focuses on institutions within non-state arenas but does not fully consider the existence of competing arenas of authority. Finally, the fourth explores how membership in multiple communities shapes individuals' lived experiences but pays little attention to institutional arrangements. All of the existing studies of politics and development thus point, more or less, to the importance of competing arenas of authority and the social institutions within them. However, they do not provide a unified language and overarching perspective required for knowledge accumulation and development programming.

2.1 Conventional State-Centric Approach

Most political scientists and development practitioners privilege the state. Early modernization theorists (e.g., Lerner, 1958; Lipset, 1959; Rustow, 1970) presumed the state seeks, and ultimately will achieve and maintain, the monopoly over the legitimate use of force in a given territory, providing security and welfare to people therein.[5] The state is the locus of participation and representation, the engine of economic growth and development (Gerschenkron, 1952). In general, these scholars argued that individuals in 'traditional' societies held values that constrained their demands on authorities and the state (Almond and Verba, 1963; Lerner, 1958). Economic development – including the spread of

---

[5] Conceptually, the state is defined as the set of individuals and organizations that holds power to control the population and resources in a given territory (Fukuyama, 2004; Nordlinger, 1981).

roads, radios, and other aspects of modernization – would lead to greater mobility, expectations, and demands for democracy, which in turn would foster development. There would be hurdles. Huntington (1968) famously argued that the strength of state institutions must keep pace with the level of social mobilization in order to avoid political decay and disorder. Yet, in general, development and democracy went hand in hand, and the state and its institutions were key. The state had the inherent ability to be more organized, technologically savvy, and capable of extending its power than social counterparts, putting them on the defensive. Where the state was not yet dominant, it would – or at least *should* – be so in the future. The question was when.

Contemporary scholars largely reject modernization theory's teleological perspective, and yet many continue to privilege the state. It is by now well-recognized that the state extends power unevenly and often fails to act as early scholars predicted (e.g., Migdal, 1988; Scott, 1972). Nevertheless, many view a high-capacity state as vital for economic growth and human development (see Cingolani, 2018 for a review). State institutions are also key: regime types affect political stability, economic growth, and human development; electoral systems shape voter behaviour, representation, policymaking, and economic welfare; administrative arrangements affect service delivery.[6] Research in this tradition has led to important insights about the logic of institutional arrangements that can be extended to other arenas of authority as well. Yet, these lessons are often overlooked because scholars in this tradition tend to view forces outside the state as disruptive. They label their impact 'corruption', 'clientelism', or 'low quality government',[7] and invest their time and energy into determining how state institutions (through the implementation of gender quotas, civil service exams, etc.) can overcome such forces.

Development practitioners also focus on state institutions. Particularly in the early 2000s, many explicitly called for state-building interventions. A report prepared for the UK's Department for International Development noted, 'The need to better understand state-building is not an academic exercise; states are crucially important to the future of those who live under their jurisdiction'

---

[6] On the role of regime type on political stability, see Geddes et al. (2018), Knutsen and Nygård (2015), Magaloni (2008), and Smith (2005); on economic growth, see Doucouliagos and Ulubaşoğlu (2008), Gerring et al. (2005), and Przeworski (2000); and on human development, see Acemoglu and Robinson (2012) and Andrews et al. (2017). On electoral systems and voter behaviour, see Bowler et al. (2001), Carey and Shugart (1995), Cox (1997; 2015), Jackman (1987), and Sanz (2017); on representation, see Krook (2018) and Norris (1997); on policy-making and economic welfare, see Carey and Hix (2013) for a short review; Kam et al. (2020). On how administrative arrangements affect service delivery, see Ahmad et al. (2005), Arends (2020), and Bardhan and Mookherjee (2006).

[7] This approach is evident even among scholars who recognize the variation in these practices. See Ledeneva (2008).

(Whaites, 2008, p. 3). Prior to becoming president of Afghanistan, but after serving as finance minister and in the World Bank, Ashraf Ghani and his co-author, Clare Lockhart, wrote a book calling for greater attention to state-building (Ghani and Lockhart, 2009). In light of spectacular failures in Afghanistan, Iraq, and elsewhere, the notion that external actors could success-fully build states came under attack (e.g., Krasner, 2011), and 'state-building' became a dirty word. Nevertheless, practitioners continued to see the strength-ening of 'core government functions' and other aspects of the state as the key to development, particularly in fragile and conflict-affected states (UNDP and World Bank, 2017).

Consequently, most programming is centred around the state. Major multi-lateral and bilateral development organizations, themselves instruments of states, often focus their programming on state organs, implementing projects around budget support, administrative strengthening, or public infrastructure. Smaller development organizations, too, often partner with government agen-cies. Thus, even when these organizations engage business, NGOs, or other elements of civil society, they tend to do so privileging the state's perspective.[8] Indeed, strengthening the capacity of these actors and organizations to engage the state is often a fundamental goal.

The instruments used to measure governance and development are also state-centric. The Fragile States Index, developed by the Fund for Peace, seeks to measure state capacity. Extant indicators of governance and service delivery (e.g., World Governance Indicators, Quality of Government) focus primarily on participation, transparency, accountability, and other dimensions of governance with respect to the state. Participation in elections or local council meetings is measured, whereas participation in tribal primaries[9] or non-state councils is not. Moreover, most indicators are at the national level, assuming that the important variation is to be found in national-level state institutions but not in local-level social institutions. Some may view the primacy given to national-level state indicators as reflecting the ease of using available data. Yet not all conventional measures are state collected, and alternatives can exist (see Appendix A for one such alternative). Moreover, measuring governance and development with regard to state institutions not only reflects the privileging of the state, but also contributes to it. Thus, while measures of state capacity and institutions are important, it is also necessary to correct the imbalance between measures of the

---

[8] For an insightful discussion of this problem with regard to HIV/AIDs programming privileges the priorities of the state over those of local village headmen in Malawi, see Dionne (2018, chapter 6).

[9] Tribal primaries are similar to party primaries, but organized by tribes to choose their candidates. These are often well run and highly contested events.

state, of which there is abundance, and measurements of non-state arenas of authority, which are largely absent.

2.2 Conventional Society-Oriented Approach

The conventional society-oriented approach focuses on the roles of identity and social capital on political behaviour and outcomes. Scholars working in this tradition ask such questions as how such social factors shape voting, representation, and even democratization (Chandra, 2007; Posner, 2005; Putnam et al., 1994; Szwarcberg, 2012). In answering these questions, they often point to the importance of competing authorities and social institutions. However, they privilege the state and do not fully theorize competing arenas of authority or the social institutions within them.

Scholars implicitly recognize that individuals are members of multiple communities, although they do not theorize about these in terms of competing arenas of authority. For instance, Henry Hale (2004, p. 480) argues that individuals have multiple dimensions of their identity and that they use them as a 'sonar radar' to navigate their world. Posner (2005) recognized that individuals have multiple dimensions of identity (e.g., religious, race, gender), and that they select from their identity repertoires when making choices. Yet, in exploring which identity structures individuals' choices when they engage in (state-based) politics, these scholars focus primarily on the arrangement of state institutions and ethnic cleavages (see also McCauley and Posner, 2019; McLaughlin, 2007). They pay far less attention to other factors that affect the strength of different arenas of authority. That is, they privilege the state.

Similarly, scholars taking this approach acknowledge the importance of rules. For instance, scholars of ethnicity emphasize rules of reciprocity, wherein they are expected to favour coethnics over non-coethnics (Björkman and Svensson, 2010; Cammett and MacLean, 2014; Corstange, 2016; Habyarimana et al., 2007; Miguel and Gugerty, 2005); those of gender focus on rules of patriarchy and homophily that at least partly explain why women are less likely to stand for office, vote in elections, or seek assistance from elected officials (Benstead, 2016; Bjarnegård, 2013). So too, scholars of social capital argue that engagement fosters the development of social organizations (or communities) in which there are 'networks, norms and trust that facilitate coordination and cooperation for mutual benefit' (Putnam, 1993, p. 35). Some recognize that the extent to which members identify with these groups or are constrained by their social institutions may vary (Dulani et al., 2021; Harris, 2022). However, the vast majority of this scholarship has not focused on differences in social institutions, and instead has assumed them to be uniform.

Yet, both the strength of competing arenas of authority and the content of institutions within them can vary significantly. This is true even within similar types of communities (i.e., ethnic, religious, geographic) within the same countries. For example, the Local Governance Performance Index (LGPI) surveys fielded in Kenya, Malawi, and Zambia in 2019 find a great deal of variation in the expectations regarding reciprocity among coethnics, across both subnational geographic locations and ethnic groups (Lust et al., 2019). A framework that takes competing arenas of authority into account thus needs to consider variation in their social institutions, not to assume them to be constant.

2.3 Focus on Social Institutions

A third strand of literature highlights the importance of social institutions and increasingly recognizes variations across them. Scholars taking this approach have uncovered a number of important findings that I build on in the pages that follow. Yet, a review of this literature finds that these scholars, too, generally privilege the state and fail to consider competing, non-state arenas of authority.[10] Moreover, they lack an overarching schema that allows them to be fully in conversation with each other and to make sense of the increasingly vast literature.

Scholars taking this approach are primarily interested in how such institutions reinforce, complement, or replace formal state institutions, and they pay little attention to the competition across different arenas of authority outside the state. Helmke and Levitsky (2004, p. 727; see also 2006) define informal institutions as 'socially shared rules, usually unwritten, that are created, communicated and enforced *outside of officially sanctioned channels*' (italics mine). That is, they portray social institutions in residual terms – as *non-state*.

Even Elinor Ostrom, undoubtedly the most influential scholar to highlight institutions outside the state, takes this approach. In *Governing the Commons* (1990), she argued that communities can devise rules to solve collective action problems and manage community resources in the absence of the state. She highlights the variation in non-state institutions, drawing attention to the importance of community boundaries, participatory decision-making, rules, enforcement, and dispute resolution mechanisms for community governance where the state is absent.[11] Yet, even in the world she describes, where local

---

[10] An important exception is found in legal scholarship. Ellickson (1994, p. 139) explicitly counters the dominant legal centralist tradition which views the state as the 'source of social order' and studies the development of social rules. His study differs from mine in that he pays greater attention to different forms of rules but less attention to competing arenas of authority outside the state.

[11] On the eight design principles for common resource management, see Ostrom (1990, pp. 90–102; 2005, p. 259).

communities have agency, the community is a single arena of authority. Furthermore, the state is still central: local solutions are particularly effective *when the state recognizes them as legitimate*. Viewing the state as the ultimate authority juxtaposed against a single local community ultimately excludes questions about competing arenas of authority outside the state.[12]

Similar tendencies are found in the writings of development specialists. Many recognize the importance of non-state actors and social institutions, but they still privilege the state and under-theorize competing arenas of authority and social institutions. The Overseas Development Institute's (ODI) Africa Power and Politics Programme (APPP) promoted the notion of 'Going with the Grain' (Kelsall, 2012), arguing that traditional authorities and local customs such as witchcraft or polygamy shape political outcomes and thus must be taken into account in development efforts (Booth and Golooba-Mutebi, 2012; Kelsall, 2008; 2012). Brian Levy (2014), then at the World Bank, argued that we could better determine which levers could help establish 'islands of effectiveness' and eventually economic growth and better governance outcomes if we take into account whether polities are dominant or competitive, and governance impartial or personalized. More recently, Matt Andrews, Lant Pritchett, and Michael Woolcock (2017) pushed even more strongly for an incremental approach to development that would consider contextual factors.

Yet even advocates of context-sensitive programming present typologies based on distinctions across state institutions – the mechanisms for centralizing rents and policy orientation for ODI's APPP and competitiveness of politics and impartiality for Levy. They question the dominance of the Weberian arrangements but nevertheless view social institutions and actors as inferior, at best, and disruptive, at worst. They explain differences between outcomes that 'should be' according to state organizational rules and those that 'are' in terms of organizational capacity of state institutions (Andrews et al., 2017, pp. 47–8). In doing so, they are unable to give guidance on how to determine which arenas of authority have weight and the impact that variations in their social institutions may have.

These gaps are evident when scholars and practitioners partner with each other, attempting to understand why interventions are more effective in some

---

[12] Subsequent work on polycentric governance (e.g., Ostrom, 2005; 2010; Ostrom and Janssen, 2004; Ostrom et al., 1961) does not overcome this problem. This model views governance as a 'complex combination' of multiple levels (e.g., local, state, national) that includes public, private, and voluntary sectors with 'overlapping realms of responsibility and functional capacities' (McGinnis and Ostrom, 2011, p. 15), and it considers how actors within various sectors are guided by institutions within them. However, it does not fully explore how arenas of authority give meaning to choices facing individuals, how individuals respond when arenas compete for their allegiance, or how the social institutions within them shape their actions.

communities than others. Micro-level approaches that focus on institutions lend themselves to increasingly sophisticated, systematic studies of their effects, particularly through randomized control trials (RCTs). Despite enormous investments of time, money, and intellect, however, the main takeaway of efforts to date has been that development programmes often travel poorly across time and space (Andrews et al., 2017; Dunning et al., 2019; Raffler et al., 2020).

Efforts to understand why have yielded a vibrant, cross-disciplinary literature examining various aspects of social institutions. Some point to networks and social ties, considering how the strength of social ties in communities affect political participation, accountability, and service provision. Others examine the institutional rules that shape interactions between groups: altruism and reciprocity, group boundaries, lineage practices, or rules with regard to specific outcomes, such as conflict mediation.[13] Still others focus on how different types of authorities influence voting, representation, or service provision (Baldwin, 2016; Díaz-Cayeros et al., 2014).

These studies provide important insights into arenas of authority and social institutions, but they are not unified by a common theoretical framework and language. This makes it remarkably difficult to compare findings across studies or draw together lessons offered by various scholars. Studies of networks and social density, for instance, tend to assume rather than interrogate the form of institutional rules that shape behaviour. Individuals from families, ethnic groups, or villages are uniformly expected to reciprocate with in-group members, or to view each other as sharing preferences and thus be more likely to coordinate. Those focused on differences in rules (e.g., reciprocity, inheritance) overlook differences in the strength of institutions. Moreover, these studies generally focus on one set of institutions, practices, or outcomes, failing to take into account how individuals may be subject to more than one arena of authority. They call for guidance on which arenas gain primacy and how social institutions within them interact to shape outcomes.

2.4 Focus on Membership in Multiple Communities

A fourth approach steps away from the state-centric, single-arena approach that underpins most work on governance and development. Both scholars working on hybridity of governance and those studying intersectionality recognize that

---

[13] On the strength of social ties, see Arias et al. (2019), Aspinall and Sukmajati (2016), Cruz et al. (2020), Ferrali et al. (2019), Jöst and Lust (2021), and Putnam (2000). Regarding different rules, see Ambec (2008), Bowles et al. (2003), and Lawson and Greene (2014) on altruism and reciprocity; Kruks-Wisner (2018) and Lieberman (2009) on group boundaries; Berge et al. (2014), Brulé and Gaikwad (2021), and Robinson and Gottlieb (2019) on lineage practices; and Fearon and Laitin (1996) on conflict mediation.

individuals act within various, competing arenas of authority, and they pay great attention to how these arenas affect the distribution of power across actors. These scholars thus provide an important critique of the dominant approaches and a basis for advocacy. However, they do not offer guidance on how competing arenas of authority or the institutions within them affect the choices individuals make and the outcomes that ensue.

Most theorists of hybridity reject binaries of state and non-state actors, traditional and modern, local and international. They examine a range of governance processes, from dispute resolution and peacebuilding to welfare provision. Importantly, they argue that governance outcomes are 'never simply a mix of two otherwise pure forms, but are perennially ongoing processes of amalgamation and dissolution' (Albrecht and Wiuff Moe, 2015, p. 5). They produce what Galvan (1997) calls 'institutional syncretism', in which structures from different arenas (as I call them) are transformed and combined to create new institutions. This view recognizes the importance of various arenas, but it sees them in terms of synthesis, rather than competition. Other scholars recognize the competition among various arenas. As Cleaver, Franks, Maganga, and Hall (2013, p. 167) argue, '"Real governance" is formed, negotiated, and contested in the street, the clinic, the market and the press as well as in the formalized public decision-making arenas of community and local government.' This view of governance as 'institutional bricolage' sees governance as shaped by multiple arenas and related institutions, but it does not seek to explore the impact of arenas and related institutions, systematically.

The study of intersectionality also acknowledges the importance of multiple communities which place demands upon and shape individuals' actions. Intersectionality grew out of feminist theories of gender and race, bringing to the fore the insight that women (and others) are members of multiple communities and subject to various power structures. As Kimberlé Crenshaw (1990) argued, the dominant conceptions of discrimination and inequality portrayed disadvantage as located on a single axis (e.g., class, race, *or* gender) and thus ignored important intra-group differences. African American and Caucasian women are all women, but African American women are doubly disadvantaged, subordinate in both class and race. The power dynamics of gender, class, race, and other communities that come into play yield experiences that are distinct – not simply the additive experience of various discriminations (Cho et al., 2013; Settles and Buchanan, 2014). Scholars of intersectionality thus emphasize lived experiences and explore how individuals' multiple identities affect their experience with discrimination and inequality. Competing arenas of authority are at work in many of these analyses, although not explicitly recognized as such. Acker (2012), for instance, gives the example of hiring practices which have assumptions that may be based on race, class, and gender; Anthias (2013) points to societal arenas, considering inequalities of women within the public domain, as well as within their own families.

These approaches yield important lessons, but they stop short of providing guidance on how to determine which arenas of authority are salient, and to what effect. Scholars of hybridity and intersectionality point to how individuals' membership in different communities affects their power and experience. However, by emphasizing the complexity of institutions, they do not provide guidance to determine which arenas of authority (or communities) matter, when. Nor do they pay explicit attention to the social institutions within these arenas. Moreover, many working in this vein resist the development of a positivist framework. For some, the goal is descriptive, not prescriptive. It is to understand the hybrid nature of governance, the ways in which power is embedded within it, and how it is shaped and reshaped. They provide an important tool for greater understanding and advocacy (e.g., Cleaver et al., 2013; Forsyth et al., 2017; Ginty and Richmond, 2016) but not a framework that helps reconcile extant findings, guide future research, and inform development actors.

2.5 Conclusion

The perspective that I present in this Element – that politics and development outcomes are the result of individuals' everyday choices, shaped by multiple, competing arenas of authority and the institutions within them – draws upon and extends decades of scholarship on politics and development. However, I make three conceptual moves that, taken together, distinguish this from previous frameworks. First, I argue that the seemingly political decisions that individuals make often have multiple meanings (Wedeen, 2002) and that individuals associate their choices with arenas of authority and attendant communities. Second, I set arenas of authority associated with different communities and the state on equal theoretical footing. Third, I emphasize the importance of institutional variation in both the state and various non-state arenas of authority. By doing so, I develop a framework that brings disparate literature into conversation, fosters knowledge accumulation, and facilitates a new approach to the study of, and programming around, politics and development.

3 Conceptualizing Arenas of Authority and Social Institutions

Understanding political behaviour and development requires that *arenas of authorities* and *social institutions* are defined in positive terms rather than as residual categories. Thus, in Sections 3.1 and 3.2, I define these concepts and describe their attributes. I begin by defining arenas of authority and then turn to social institutions and their constituent parts: roles, rules, and rewards. In Section 3.3, I examine the relative stability of social institutions. Social institutions evolve, and they do so at least partly in response to socio-economic conditions. Yet, they are sticky. They do not simply reflect social and economic factors, nor do they change too quickly for actors to take them into account when making decisions. Thus, they can be analytically useful in crafting theories of behaviour and development and should be taken into account in policymaking and programming.

3.1 Arenas of Authority

An *arena of authority* is a sphere of activity with clear membership, goals, and institutions. Visualize an arena of authority as a physical arena. It has boundaries, which distinguish members of the community (inside the arena) from outsiders. Membership in the community may be based on such foundations as ethnicity, tribe, or religion, but regardless of the foundation, the community seeks to propagate itself beyond the current generation. This common goal does not imply equality or a lack of conflict. The community may be highly differentiated, with leaders and followers, masters and slaves. Indeed, members need not necessarily have joined the community by volition. Members may also contest the rules or compete with each other over resources. Ultimately, however, those within the arena of authority are engaged, more or less consciously, in a grand project of sustaining the group. They are thus mutually interdependent, with each member's welfare tied to that of others within the arena.

Like the state,[14] social arenas of authority govern much of individuals' lives, from cradle to grave. They regulate marriage and biological reproduction, raise resources for community goods, provide welfare, and resolve disputes. Indeed, in much of the world, the vast majority of individuals take civil and criminal cases before customary venues or nowhere at all, and public confidence is often higher in such venues than in their state counterparts (Gutmann and Voigt, 2020; Logan, 2013). Some striking statistics: rural Liberians took only about 4 per cent of cases involving economic disputes and 8 per cent of those involving violent crimes to the state courts, compared to 36 per cent and 40 per cent, respectively, to customary courts (Sandefur and Siddiqi, 2013, p. 42);[15] Indonesians were equally likely to take cases to customary or state courts, but

---

[14] Indeed, one could view the state simply as one among many arenas of authority.

[15] Most rural Liberians did not take grievances to any venue. It is important to note that these figures actually understate the role of non-state arenas of authority in dispute resolution and land access. As illustrated in the Introduction, individuals' engagement in 'state' institutions is often driven by their positions in non-state arenas of authority and attendant social institutions.

they have much higher confidence in the customary courts (Harper, 2011); and increasing numbers of Muslims in Germany opt to register marriage, divorce, and solve disputes in sharia' courts unrecognized by the state (Jaraba, 2020). Much of the world's population also relies on social arenas for access to land. Indeed, in 2017, the World Bank (2017) reported that only about 30 per cent of the world's population had state titles to their land. This is despite decades-long global efforts at state land titling, in a state-centric attempt to increase legibility, extend state control, and (arguably) foster economic growth and equity.[16]

Arenas of authority have boundaries. Boundaries separate those who are within the community from outsiders, and they are more or less porous. Some arenas tightly restrict who may enter or leave the community. Children born to a Jewish mother are Jewish, while those born to a Muslim father are Muslim – or at least they should be according to membership rules in Judaism and Islam. Ethnic groups can be similar, particularly if one defines ethnicity as Kanchan Chandra (2006, p. 398) does: 'a subset of identity categories in which eligibility for membership is determined by attributes associated with, or believed to be associated with, descent (described here simply as descent-based attributes)'. In the middle of the spectrum are groups in which not all individuals are eligible for entry and exit may be difficult, but not impossible. Consider members of campus Greek societies and inner-city gangs. Fraternities admit students but not 'townies', and gangs often admit individuals from certain areas and demographic groups but not others. At the other extreme are arenas with porous boundaries. Take for example some neighbourhoods or open religious congregations. One might become a resident in a neighbourhood simply by moving into a community, a congregational member by converting.

It may be tempting to associate the porousness of boundaries with the type of community – to view geographic communities as relatively open, ethnic, or sectarian groups as closed. Yet, there is considerable variation in membership rules within the same type of arena, across both space and time. For instance, upper-class, white Americans may face few barriers to accessing any neighbourhood, at least financially; however, the same is not true for their less-wealthy counterparts or for African Americans in the 1950s, for whom redlining practices limited their ability to enter certain housing markets.[17] It is also not true elsewhere in the world. In parts of Ghana, Oman, and Zambia, for instance,

---

[16] There is a vibrant debate over whether land titling promotes or undermines land tenure security and equality, particularly for women and the poor. See concerns raised by Jones-Casey and Knox (2011) and Obeng-Odoom (2015).

[17] For more on how redlining limited housing access for African Americans, see the HOCL federal lending program in the 1930s (https://dsl.richmond.edu/panorama/redlining/#loc=11/43.018/-83.734&city=flint-mi). It is a fascinating, albeit depressing, reflection of how group boundaries were both incorporated into and reinforced by state public policy.

permission of traditional authorities is often required for one to obtain land in their area. So too of religious communities. In some cases, one can change religion as easily as clothing styles, leaving one arena to join another. Elsewhere, this is not the case. One does not simply convert from Sunni Islam to Shi'ism, yet alone to Christianity, in much of the Middle East, nor revoke membership within Hindu or Muslim communities in much of India and Pakistan. The costs of attempting to exit the arena are high, bearing at times even the penalty of death, and the ability to enter other arenas is limited.

Finally, social arenas, like states, seek a degree of sovereignty. Sovereignty is generally associated with states, defined as the supreme authority over a polity within an established territory. Yet, substantively, the key to sovereignty is the supreme legitimate authority over a polity. As Agnew (2005, p. 441) argues, such '*effective sovereignty is not necessarily predicated on and defined by the strict and fixed boundaries of individual states*'. Indeed, political authority is neither exclusively territorial nor restricted to states. Arenas of authority seek ultimate, legitimate authority over activities that are key to their community's survival. As examples, Lebanese religious sects seek to maintain control over marriage, divorce, and other family matters; Malawian ethnic groups aim to control rules governing inheritance, authority, and land rights.

Both states and arenas of authority seek sovereignty, but the nature of sovereignty the state requires may differ from that sought by social arenas. Here it is useful to recall Jackson and Rosberg's (1984) distinction between empirical and juridical statehood in sub-Saharan Africa. Empirical statehood is based on the exercise of power – the monopoly of the legitimate use of force on populations within a territorial entity – and it exercises power with an eye inward, towards the national population. Juridical statehood is based on international recognition, and its aim is to be included in the international society of states. In the modern era, states maintain themselves by obtaining de jure recognition. Arenas of authority neither necessarily require nor receive such recognition. They seek de facto power over the issues that are critical to their community (an issue we will return to in Section 4), and they vary in the extent to which this requires territorial control.

These competing aspirations for sovereignty open a range of possibilities for the relations between states and other arenas. At times, conflict is inevitable. Individuals located simultaneously in these overlapping arenas can comply with one authority only if they fail to comply with another. ISIS and states in the West provide a striking example of this. The estimated 20,000 foreigners who fought on behalf of ISIS in Syria and Iraq could only respond to ISIS' authority by opposing that of their home states, effectively committing treason. At other times, states can cede authority over individuals, or over some spheres of their social and economic activities. Joel Migdal (1988) highlighted the fact that states often do so when they are incapable of maintaining rule or unwilling to expend resources necessary to control populations or territory. This occurs not only when states are weak but also when they are strong – as seen in governments' hesitance to enter inner-city 'ghettos' of the United States (Sampson et al., 1999) and marginalized suburbs in Sweden (Esaiasson and Sohlberg, 2020).

Before turning to the institutions within these arenas, note that not all entities outside the state are social arenas. Non-profit organizations and corporations often have more limited goals. They aim to produce widgets, garner profits, and maybe even ensure the longevity of the enterprise. They can benefit from and thus may seek to develop the community's skills. But they do not aim to govern the community. Reebok may care what its employees wear on their feet and seek customer loyalty over Adidas, but their board – most likely – cares little about who they marry and how they live. Where they do (e.g., family businesses, company towns), the economic system is better understood as an arena of authority than an organization. Indeed, markets and class-based systems are arenas of authority. However, organizations, as entities, that work unproblematically (save, at least, for illegal enterprises) with and under the state as well as other arenas of authority, and do not compete over individuals' allegiances, are not. (See Table 1 for a summary.)

3.2 Defining Social Institutions

Social institutions structure engagement within arenas of authority. Sociologists debate the definition of social institutions perhaps as much as political scientists tangle over how to conceptualize the state (Miller, 2019). Some scholars define social institutions narrowly, such that they refer to the rules that govern actions and the rewards or punishments associated with compliance – a view of institutions in accordance with that of the Nobel Prize-winning economist Douglas North (1990), among others. Yet, rules invoked are often role-dependent, varying according to the position that one holds in the community. Moreover, even when enforced, the impact of various rules depends on the magnitude of costs or benefits associated with compliance. To highlight this, I define *social institutions* as the *roles, rules,* and *rewards* that structure activities within a community as it attempts to govern and ensure its survival.[18] Social institutions

---

[18] This is in line with Turner (1997, p. 6), who defines social institutions as 'a complex of positions, roles, norms and values lodged in particular types of social structures and organizing relatively stable patterns of human activity with respect to fundamental problems in producing life-sustaining resources, in reproducing individuals, and in sustaining viable societal structures within a given environment'. It is also similar to Ostrom's description of 'action situations', which are 'characterized using seven clusters of variables: (1) participants (who may be either

Table 1 Comparing social arenas, the state, and other organizations

Characteristics	Social Arenas	State	Organizations
Goals	Reproduction of the community: maintain order, provide services and security, enforce decisions	Reproduction of the community: maintain order, provide services and security, enforce decisions	Limited ambition: organizational output or profit
Community Membership/ Boundaries	Range of porousness	Generally, less porous	Generally, more porous
Territory	Geographic or non-geographic	Geographic	Non-geographic
Sovereignty	Required	Required	Not required
Recognition: key to sovereignty	Empirical (de facto)	Internationally recognized, juridical (de jure)	Nationally recognized, juridical (de jure)

determine individuals' positions within a community, the actions available to them and others, and the consequences thereof. In doing so, they affect the distribution of power in the community, members' expectations of the others' responses, and consequently, individuals' decisions. (See Table 2 for a summary.)

Because arenas of authority are multifaceted, the social institutions within them regulate a range of needs. These extend beyond the issue around which the community is formed. For instance, social institutions within ethnic arenas of authority determine not only who belongs (kinship), but also who has access to land and other resources (the economy), who has the right to rule the community (government), and what knowledge is passed down, when, and to whom (education). Institutions within religious communities regulate not only the relationship between members and their god (religion), but also tithing and charity (the economy), marriage and reproduction (kinship).

---

single individuals or corporate actors), (2) positions, (3) potential outcomes, (4) action-outcome linkages, (5) the control that participants exercise, (6) types of information generated, and (7) the costs and benefits assigned to actions and outcomes' (Ostrom, 2005, p. 14).

Table 2 Components of social institutions

Dimension	Definition
Roles	Positions with associated rights and responsibilities, and rewards that follow
Rules	Explicit or implied codes outlining *who* is *permitted or required to/not to* take an *action*, within *specific conditions,* and with *expected sanctions or rewards* for *compliance or noncompliance*
Rewards	The consequences of acting in compliance or non-compliance with understood rules, including both positive inducements and sanctions.

Within each arena, individuals assume roles. These are the positions that members of the community can hold, distinct from the individuals who hold them. Roles are associated with rights and responsibilities, and the rewards that follow. To simplify, there are leaders and members. In religious or kinship systems, for instance, these are priests and parishioners, imams and followers, chiefs and subjects, elders and youths. The ability to access different positions may depend on gender, age, bloodline, or other qualities. Where these characteristics shape roles within arenas of authority, we can understand them as gendered, ageist, or ethnic, respectively. Yet, such characteristics as gender, age, or ethnicity are not arenas of authority in and of themselves. Arenas of authority are associated with an identity group that defines the community, but not every identity group constitutes a community that defines an arena of authority.

The roles that men and women, the elderly and young, or those of different bloodlines are allowed to occupy vary across time, and across arenas. Again, this is true even in communities founded on similar bases. Consider the relationship between gender and leadership roles in religious arenas. In most religions, women are subordinate to men, barred from taking the highest leadership roles. Yet this varies across religions, and even within them. For instance, while most Protestant Christian religions allow the ordination of women, the Southern Baptist Convention, which constitutes the largest protestant denomination in the United States, bars women from the highest positions and promotes distinct gender roles in the household, encouraging women to submit to their husbands' leadership (Crary, 2019). Gender roles also vary across time. The Catholic Church, for example, prohibited women from any formal leadership roles until January 2021, when Pope Francis amended Canon Law to allow women to act in leadership roles played by lay leaders (e.g., altar servers or readers) (Povoledo, 2021).

Rules determine who may assume certain roles, as well as who can enter the community and obligations of those within it. Think of rules as statements that determine *who* is *permitted or required to/not to* take an action, within specific conditions, and with expected sanctions or rewards for compliance/non-compliance.[19] Rules set forth expectations and implications, but they allow individual choice. It is true that an individual does not get to choose 'on what' they act (i.e., whether or not there is a rule regarding the choice at hand) or the consequences of their actions, but they decide what action to take.

Finally, social institutions entail the rewards and consequences of actions. John Harsanyi writes that 'People's behavior can be largely explained in terms of two dominant interests: economic gain and social acceptance' (1969, p. 524). Both come in the forms of carrots and sticks. Individuals may receive bonuses or economic rewards, or face fines or material losses. They may enjoy respect and moral standing or face social shaming and ostracization.

Roles, rules, and rewards combine to shape the choices and actions that are the core of politics and development. Coercive power has long been held as the key motivation for compliance with state authority, spanning from Hobbes and Mill to modern theorists, such as Tyler (2006). Scholars recognize that coercive power, or carrots and sticks, may motivate actors with regard to non-state leaders as well (see Scott, 1972, or Mares and Young, 2016). But desire to do the right thing may as well. Individuals may respond to calls for action because they believe that it is right and proper to do so (Lipset, 1959, p. 71). In this case, they contribute regardless of other's abilities to reward or sanction (Beetham, 1991; Kelman and Hamilton, 1989; Sparks et al., 1996; Sunshine and Tyler, 2003; Tyler, 1990).

Before discussing the stability of arenas of authority and social institutions, it is important to clarify what social institutions are *not*. Social institutions are not culture – if culture is defined as beliefs and preferences – even if culture includes preferences over political outcomes or policies (e.g., Almond and Verba, 1965; Inglehart and Welzel, 2005).[20] Expressed preferences may reflect social institutions, as individuals may develop or choose to reveal preferences

---

[19] This formula draws from Ostrom (2005, p. 187), who puts it slightly differently: 'ATTRIBUTES of participants who are OBLIGED, FORBIDDEN, OR PERMITTED to ACT (or AFFECT an outcome) under specified CONDITIONS, OR ELSE'.

[20] The approach I set forth shares more in common with the notion of culture as set forth in Chabal and Daloz (2006), who define culture as 'an environment, a constantly evolving setting, within which human behaviour follows a number of particular courses' (p. 21) or a 'system of meanings'. Their approach focuses on a single 'culture' and has interpretivist underpinnings, while the perspective I present here examines competing arenas and has institutionalist foundations.

that are in accordance with social rules in order to avoid repercussions. However, preferences should not be confused with the rules that shape them. Social institutions, like social norms, are also not simply reactive instincts or habits, like quieting a crying baby or writing a diary (Bell and Cox, 2015; Legros and Cislaghi, 2020). Social institutions entail a set of obligations and consequences. In this respect, social institutions are similar to injunctive norms, although not to descriptive ones. However, as Legros and Cislaghi (2020) show, there are multiple, and at times incompatible, understandings of 'social norms'. Thus, for clarity, I focus on social institutions defined in terms of roles, rules, and rewards.

Finally, and importantly, social institutions are not simply informal institutions. Scholars and practitioners tend to equate state rules with formal institutions, and those outside the state with informal ones. Yet the rules in social institutions can be formal (where formal is understood as explicitly stated, parchment institutions) or even change in their degree of formality over time. Moreover, as Samuel Bowles (2016) argues, such codification may, itself, influence the outcomes. Only by distinguishing between formal and informal rules in social institutions can we explore the effect of formalization.[21]

3.3 The Stability of Arenas of Authority and Social Institutions

Arenas of authority and social institutions within them need to be relatively stable and not simply reflect other underlying factors if they are to form the basis of a useful approach to understanding political behaviour and development outcomes. Communities develop social institutions as they seek to govern themselves, and they do so in response to specific challenges their context raises. Consequently, one of the thorniest issues in the study of authority and institutions is separating their effects from the factors that give rise to them. If social institutions simply reflect existing conditions, then one cannot assess their impact independently from these conditions (e.g., address endogeneity issues). However, there is good reason to believe that although arenas and social institutions are neither exogenously determined nor static, they are relatively stable and, over time, may become divorced from their initial purpose. They thus provide useful leverage for research and programming.

Evolutionary biologists, cultural anthropologists, economists, and psychologists have argued that norms develop as a mechanism to ensure a group's survival (Bowles et al., 2003). These may be shaped partly by ecological conditions.

---

[21] Samuel Bowles (2016) makes a compelling argument that creating formal laws and clearly defined sanctions can undermine goodwill and better outcomes. Many of the studies which he draws upon, however, have changed incentives and formality at the same time. Important questions about the impact of formalization alone remain.

For instance, Harry Triandis (1989, p. 510), a pioneer in cross-cultural psychology, argues that thinly populated areas were more likely to develop individualist cultures; since '[o]ne can scarcely reject a neighbour if one has only one neighbour', those living in sparsely populated areas came to accept a great deal of diversity. Economic institutions may also influence social institutions. Joseph Henrich and colleagues' (2001) masterful study of reciprocity in fifteen small communities – across twelve countries on five continents – found that how much people rely on market exchange in their daily lives and the level of cooperation required for economic production affected the levels of cooperation in lab-in-the-field games. People who were nearly self-sufficient and engaged in small-scale production, such as those living on family-based farms in Peru or Bolivia, were much less likely to cooperate. In contrast, Indonesians who relied primarily on large-scale whale fishing – where more than a dozen men may set out in a large canoe to hunt whale – were much more likely to cooperate. These findings are in line with Lauren MacLean's (2010, chapter 6) study of reciprocity in Ghana and Cote d'Ivoire. She finds that the shift from cocoa to tomato farming expanded the scope of social ties and made relations more diffuse in Ghana, while the failure to make such a shift led to reciprocal relations that were stronger but also more concentrated among a smaller family group in Cote d'Ivoire.

Institutions are continually contested and evolving, but they are also sticky. Forces such as urbanization, technological changes, ageing populations, and efforts aimed at shaping societies through rules aimed at ending ethnic, sexual, or gender discrimination are all catalysts for change. Nevertheless, institutions outlast the conditions that gave rise to them, despite constant pressures (Bowles et al., 2003). Moreover, the constellation of roles and rules that define social institutions shape the distribution of power. Thus, a change in a single rule that may disrupt the balance of power is often countered by other rules. Rubie Watson (1990, p. 241) illustrates this with regard to inheritance laws. She argues that the change to partible inheritance, or the division of land equally among offspring in the family, led to downward mobility in China but not in Europe because partible inheritance in Europe was coupled with rules that promoted late marriage, close-kin marriage, and marriage within class. In short, institutions are sticky.

More importantly for the purpose here, individuals making decisions – whether to run in elections and whom to support, whether to contribute to community funds, or whom to turn to in resolving disputes – generally make their choices in the context of relatively legible and stable institutions. When they do not – when technological, environmental, medical, or other changes heighten uncertainty – it is possible to consider the range of outcomes they expect, still taking into account their perception of social institutions. Political scientists should be concerned about endogeneity issues, cautioned against attributing causal influence to institutions or assuming that thorny political problems can be solved through (re)designing state institutions. However, there is much to be gained by considering arenas of authority and social institutions at a given point in time. To understand decisions and subsequent outcomes from the perspective of everyday people engaged in making choices, the origins of different authority structures are of little consequence. What matters are the communities they belong to, their roles within these communities, the attendant rules and associated rewards, and the extent to which these affect the decision at hand.

4 Which Arenas Matter, When, and Why

To move away from a perspective that either routinely privileges the state or presumes ex ante that an ethnic, religious, or other arena drives individuals' decisions, analysts and practitioners need criteria by which to determine which arenas guide actions. When a working-class Catholic chooses between a pro-union, abortion rights candidate and a pro-business, anti-abortion one, how do they respond to the expectations of and pressures within their religious community and union? So, too, as a parliamentarian decides whether to place a new clinic in their home village or a more populated town where votes are more plentiful, how do they weigh obligations to their local community, which expects priority from 'their' MP, and their political party, which seeks future votes? In this section, I argue that we gain traction on these questions by considering the *salience* of the issue at hand for the community within each arena, the *strength* of the relevant arenas over the individual, and their *shape* – or, whether or not the social institutions in salient arenas of authority are congruent.

4.1 Salience of Arenas

The first challenge is to determine which arenas of authority are associated with the issues in question. Two factors come into play. First is the extent to which the issue is salient to fundamental tenants of the community, and thus salient to the community's imperative to maintain itself. Second is the extent to which elites within an arena use the issue to extend their power vis-à-vis competing elites from other arenas.

To understand whether individuals see the issue at hand as relevant to the community, Kate Baldwin, Kristen Kao, and Ellen Lust find value in the notion of domain congruence.[22] Domain congruence reflects the extent to which an issue or activity and the arena of authority are related. If individuals believe that the community cares deeply about the issue, they are more likely to expect that leaders and community members will expend resources to sanction noncompliance. Non-coercive power is also likely to be higher when there is greater domain congruency. Citizens may view it as more normatively appropriate to comply with demands of authorities and other community members when the activities called for match their domain of power, or where they have greater expertise (see Presthus, 1960, p. 195 for the classic statement of this). Individuals thus should be more likely to respond to demands made when they are associated with arenas in which there is greater domain congruence.

We find evidence of this in a study of authority in Kenya, Malawi, and Zambia. The study employed a survey experiment aimed at understanding how citizens respond to requests when asked to do so by different authorities.[23] It focused on three activities (voting for an MP candidate, contributing to a school fund, and contributing to a burial fund) and sought to understand the extent to which state and traditional leaders at local and supra-local levels[24] mobilize support. We find that the relative power of leaders depends on the match between their domain (or arena of authority) and that of the activity. For instance, the MP, as a supra-local, state leader, was better placed to mobilize support for the MP candidate than to mobilize contributions to a burial or school fund. In contrast, the local councillor had greater influence on contributions to the school fund, which can be understood as a local, state-oriented activity.

Individuals view different arenas as more or less appropriate to issue areas even when they are located at the same level (e.g., are local or supra-local) or are of the same type. For instance, in a study examining when individuals comply with directives to take Covid-19-related precautionary measures, my colleagues and I found that Malawians viewed village heads as more legitimate in issuing such directives than local religious authorities. They appear to view advocating precautionary health measures as fitting within the village head's purview of maintaining community welfare – an association that may be reinforced by the

[22] Baldwin, K., Kao, K. and Lust, E. (2021). 'Is Authority Fungible? Legitimacy, Domain Congruence, and the Limits of Power in Africa'. Unpublished manuscript.

[23] ibid.

[24] The authorities included a neighbour, village head, or neighbourhood block leader, local councillor, member of parliament, and traditional authority (a customary authority located roughly at the district level).

role these village heads play in organizing immunization drives and other health initiatives (Kao et al., 2021).[25]

Issues may also be salient because they are part of a broader struggle between communities in different arenas. Elites and other community members in arenas of authority can compete with those of other arenas to gain or maintain their power. For example, they can use action-oriented issue framing to shape members' understanding of the activity, the choices at hand, and their implications. Take, for instance, dispute resolution in Jordan. Jordanian tribal codes generally demand that parties to a conflict not only accept the solution but also view it as a final reconciliation. Thus, as the head of public relations for the Jordanian Public Safety Department explains, 'Tribal customs preserve the restoration of social balance after a crime has occurred', whereas when state directives are issued, tribal processes are still required to prevent continued conflict (Watkins, 2014, p. 40). The rules guiding the tribal process imbue the outcome with a fundamentally different meaning from one reached within the state courts alone, and they help to maintain the tribal arena.

Similar dynamics are found in the West. In his study of a ranching community in northern California, Ellickson (1994, p. 60) highlights how the community maintained social order apart from the state. In part, this was done by rules that defined 'being a good neighbour' as one who sought to solve such issues as cattle poaching and breach of agreements within the community, rather than to take disputes to state courts. Thus, when deciding whether to take an issue to the state court or address it locally, the rancher not only views the choice as one over the issue itself, but also as one that signals their adherence to the ranching community.

Simply framing an issue as part of a larger goal does not necessarily ensure that members view it as salient. Social movement theorists argue that the success of such framing depends on the consistency of the message, its empirical credibility, and the credibility of its messengers (Benford and Snow, 2000). Success also depends upon the strength of competing arenas. Thachil (2014), for instance, finds that the elite-led Bharatiya Janata Party (BJP) used a combination of Hindu nationalist rhetoric and privately provided services to mobilize support from lower castes in Chhattisgarh. However, its strategy met strong resistance in Uttar Pradesh, where the Bahujan Samaj Party (BSP) had successfully won over the lower castes, thus polarizing the class divides. Even when communities use similar strategies to influence individuals' decisions, different arenas of authority may not have equal sway.

---

[25] The underlying mechanisms driving compliance also differed: compliance with the village head was associated with fear of sanctions, while compliance with the hospital head was associated with expertise.

4.2 Strength of Arenas

The influence of different arenas of authority over individuals depends on the strength of arenas. This is determined, in part, by the nature of the arena: the level of solidarity among its members, the range of aspects within individuals' lives that the arena touches, and the extent to which the community and its leadership can monitor and sanction members. Other factors are specific to individual members: the extent to which they are beholden to the community and the exit options they enjoy.

First, social solidarity strengthens arenas. Members are more likely to view obligations as legitimate when they feel themselves to be part of the community. In such cases, they are also more likely to feel they will reap benefits from their contributions when they act together. This is particularly true in small communities, where the fact that each contribution counts can help overcome collective action problems (Olson, 1965).

Two studies of India highlight the importance of solidarity. India's caste system is a well-known example of a closed social system, with caste-specific roles, rules, and rewards, and clear discrimination of the lowest cast, the Dalit or 'untouchables'. Often, there is solidarity within the castes but not across them. Timothy Waring's (2011) research on irrigation in villages of Tamil Nadu illustrates how individuals resist demands to contribute when solidarity is absent. He finds an association between the size of one's caste in a community and how much labour people volunteered to cooperative irrigation systems: individuals volunteered 77 per cent more days, on average, if the share of their caste rose from 0 to 50 per cent of the village. Moreover, lab-in-the-field experiments revealed that Dalits in Dalit-non-Dalit groups were less likely to contribute, and Dalit collaborators confirmed that 'Dalits often reduce their cooperation when called upon by high caste people, because they assume that they will not benefit from any project they are asked to support' (Waring and Bell, 2013, pp. 402–3). Yet, Prerna Singh (2011; 2015) argues that such solidarity, or what she called 'We-ness', can develop in communities even when they are divided by religion or caste. Examining Kerala, India, she argues that Keralites established a 'We-ness' based on a common language and shared Malayali culture. This allowed them to bridge religious and caste divides, support community services, and even engage effectively in the battle against the coronavirus pandemic (Singh, 2020).

Studies of race and voting also suggest that individuals respond more to demands made in arenas of authority where they feel themselves to be full members of the community. Michael Dawson (1995) argued that African Americans complied more with the demands of their racial groups than class groupings because experiences with racial discrimination led them to view their personal interest as closely tied to that of other blacks, or to have what he called 'linked fate'. Importantly, in this view, social institutions that guide the behaviour of groups in *other* arenas of authority (i.e., the rules leading non-African Americans to discriminate against out-group members) may foster solidarity within a community. Such feelings of solidarity affect the extent to which individuals vote in accordance with social institutions in racial arenas of authority. In the United States, black and Latin American respondents who expressed sentiments of linked fate were more likely to support minority candidates (Bejarano et al., 2021). In contrast, in South Africa, individuals whose appearance led them to be singled out as different, and thus experience fewer feelings of linked fate, were less likely to vote with their group (Harris, 2022).

Second, the more multifaceted the arena of authority – encompassing a wider range of behaviour and outcomes relevant to individuals' welfare – the greater its influence over individuals' choices.[26] The rewards of complying with rules within an arena relate not only to the direct act at hand, but also to the indirect consequences that come from maintaining strong relations with other members of the community. In arenas associated with a wide range of activities and future benefits – finding a job, securing one's property, obtaining help in old age – individuals have greater incentives to comply with the social institutions.

Examples abound. Frederic Schaffer (1998) finds that individuals vote in accordance with male heads of households because the costs of transgressing patriarchs (i.e., social institutions in kinship arenas) go far beyond voting day. He explains:

> The need to secure benefits for family, association, or village and the pressure to reinforce bonds of mutuality overwhelm commitment to the national public good. … Vulnerable populations that rely heavily on group cohesion for their survival may well perceive the risks of social discord occasioned by elections to be so great that the question of whether one candidate or another would serve the interests of the community is inconsequential by comparison.
>
> (pp. 98–9)

Encompassing arenas are found outside the Global South as well. Studying the United States, psychologist Paul Piff and his colleagues (Piff et al., 2010; 2012; Piff and Robinson, 2017) find that the poor are more likely to respond to social obligations around family and friendship arenas. This may be because the poor rely on neighbours as their safety net, and thus they are much more likely to expect and give assistance to each other. The American poor act much like the

---

[26] Max Gluckman's (1973, p. 19) concept of 'multiplex relationships' has similar qualities.

Ghanaians in Pankani's (2014) study discussed at the outset of this Element. Similarly, studying poor communities in England, Prisca Jöst (2021) finds evidence that the poor's voting behaviour is more closely associated with their beliefs over how others in their community vote than is the case for wealthier Brits. She argues that the poor have fewer links to individuals outside their community and thus fewer external options. Consequently, the local arena of authority is more encompassing, having a greater influence on the poor.

Encompassing arenas affect not only members, but leaders as well. Lily Tsai's influential study of service provision in China demonstrates this nicely. Tsai centres her argument around solidary groups, in which members are 'obligated to behave and judged according to the group's standards of what constitutes a good person and a good member – "good" meaning not just what is good for the group but the goodness (versus badness) of human action and character' (Tsai, 2007, p. 95). When solidary groups, which are akin to arenas of authority, encompassed all citizens in the local government jurisdiction and embedded local officials, both citizens and local officials were more responsive.

Third, arenas are stronger when leaders or other community members are more capable of monitoring and enforcement. Rules that enhance visibility foster compliance. This explains why many communities encourage contributions during weddings, public benefit auctions and other ceremonies during which behaviour is publicly observed, emotions of solidarity run high, and social sanctions are particularly effective (Ambec, 2008). Proximity facilitates monitoring as well, as it allows authorities and other community members a better vantage point for monitoring individuals. Finally, in arenas with dense social networks, in which people have a large number of ties with others in the community, information flows more swiftly through communities, and leaders and members are more likely to know of and sanction non-compliance. This role of networks may explain why individuals respond more to demands of coethnics than to non-coethnics (Habyarimana et al., 2007; Miguel and Gugerty, 2005), as well as Granovetter's (1973; 1983) finding that weak ties are more beneficial than strong ties in mobilization.

Prisca Jöst and I (2022) uncover evidence of the role of networks in a study of the poor in Kenya, Malawi, and Zambia. Using a hierarchical model that allows us to consider the relationship between community social ties and compliance, we analyse the survey experiment on authority that Kate Baldwin, Kristen Kao, and I employed (see Section 4.1). Prisca Jöst and I find that the poor are more likely to participate when asked by local traditional authorities and neighbours than they are when asked by more remote leaders, a finding that highlights the importance of proximity. Moreover, these local authorities had even greater influence over respondents living in communities with dense social ties. Higher expectations of social sanctioning in these communities appear to explain greater compliance, at least in part. Networks within communities – geographical or otherwise – facilitate monitoring and enforcement, strengthening the arena of authority.

Finally, individuals' responsiveness to different arenas of authority depends not only on the nature of the arena, but also on individuals' characteristics. To some degree, there are idiosyncratic differences in people that make them more or less likely to comply with authority – state or otherwise. Ellickson (1994, Chapter 3) describes a rancher in Shasta, California, who seemed impervious to the rules and rewards of the ranching community, for no obvious reason. However, circumstances can also systematically affect the hold that arenas have over individuals. Arenas have less influence over those who can more easily opt-out of the community or weather the costs associated with reneging on obligations. As Triandis (1989) notes, in general, more affluent and more mobile individuals can escape the watchful eye of their community; the poor and less mobile rely more on benefits accorded by compliance, and are less able to escape sanction.

This helps to explain why individuals who are disadvantaged within an arena may nevertheless turn to it, even when given the opportunity to venue shop. Justin Sandefur and Bilal Siddiqi (2013) demonstrate this in Liberia. There, women were far more likely to take their disputes to customary, rather than state, fora, even when they were aware of their alternative options, and despite the fact that customary tribunals disadvantage women. The exception was women in the process of suing men, who were more likely to file charges in state courts. However, this exception may prove the rule. In this context, it is extraordinary for women to sue men, a move afforded to those who are better able to refuse compliance with the social institutions. Expecting that alternative venues will free the disadvantaged from repressive relationships misses the fact that those most disadvantaged are often least well-positioned to escape the arena of authority.

4.3 Shaping the Decision Field: Institutional Congruence *versus* Identity Cleavages

The discussion so far has focused on the factors that strengthen arenas, at times leading one to dominate another. In reality, however, people are members of numerous arenas, some of which may dictate the same action when choices are set before them. Where this is the case, individuals may behave in accordance with social institutions of multiple arenas, none of which is – by itself – the strongest. Thus, what matters in determining how arenas come together to shape an individual's choice is how social institutions within these arenas overlap, not how membership does.

Scholars of identity and politics have focused on the latter: the overlap in membership, or put differently, identity cleavage structures. Some emphasize nested groups, focusing on cases in which individuals in one community are subsumed in a larger community (e.g., members in a locality are all members of a larger region) and asking which groups individuals respond to most (Lawler, 1992; Lawler et al., 2016). Others are particularly interested in how cleavage structures affect outcomes such as conflict (Gordon et al., 2015), democratization (Deutsch, 1961; Lijphart, 1977; Lipset, 1959; 1960), and economic growth (Selway, 2011).

These scholars emphasize different social arrangements, but they largely agree that what matters is how these different identity-based communities influence individuals. Taylor and Rae (1969, p. 534) refer to the different 'political norms', associated with an individual's membership in different groups, that lead the individual to be 'cross-pressured'. Lipset (1960, p. 88) emphasizes the 'multiple and politically inconsistent affiliations, loyalties and *stimuli*' (my italics) that individuals face. Lawler and colleagues (2016, p. 149) point to 'nested group commitments' which can at times be in conflict – as the example of Dalits in Tamil Nadu illustrated.

However, the cleavage structure of identity groups does not necessarily correspond to the overlap of social institutions within them. Identity groups may be nested and yet make competing demands on their members. At the same time, identity cleavages may be cross-cutting and yet require the member to make the same choice.

To understand this, consider the Ghanaian bureaucrat presented in the introduction. The bureaucrat had spied her chief standing in the office queue, waiting to process his papers, and led him to the front of the line. This response would be consistent with the constellation of rules in Scenario 1, presented in Table 3. In this case, the bureaucrat is a member of the state, her ethnic group, and her kinship group. She recognizes that the administrative rules require her to treat applicants in the order they arrive, but social institutions within her ethnic arena as well as those within her more immediate kin arena require her to serve the elder first. In the absence of strong state institutions, she does so. In the second scenario, however, she may make a very different choice. The institutions associated with the state and ethnic arenas remain the same. However, imagine she comes from a very nationalist family, so rules in her kin arena require her to uphold state rules. Now, even if the ethnic arena has the single largest hold (e.g., she anticipates good standing in her ethnic group affects her ability to get other jobs or marry well), she may still require the chief to wait his turn. She does so

Table 3 Arenas of authority, social institutions, and choices

Scenario	Arena of Authority	Social Institution: Rule	Prescribed Choice	Outcome
Scenario 1	State	Treat applications in order received	*Do not* give chief preferential service	*Give* chief preferential service
	Ethnic	Treat coethnic elders with respect	*Give* chief preferential service	
	Kinship	Act reciprocally towards kin in times of need	*Give* chief preferential service	
Scenario 2	State	Treat applications in order received	*Do not* give chief preferential service	*Do not* give chief preferential service
	Ethnic	Treat coethnic elders with respect	*Give* chief preferential service	
	Kinship	Respect state institutions	*Do not* give chief preferential service	

when there is a congruence of rules between the state and kinship arenas, and when they are jointly stronger than her ethnic arena.

4.4 Illustration: Subnational Variation in Jordanian Electoral Participation

Before turning to social institutions in greater detail, I want to illustrate the points set forth thus far by examining electoral participation in Jordan. The case demonstrates variation in the strength of arenas of authority based on kinship, religion, and state, and shows how differences in these arenas and individuals' reliance shape the influence of different arenas over their electoral behavior. Moreover, the case illustrates how subnational variation in the strength of these arenas affects electoral participation – in particular, why Jordanians living in rural areas have been much more likely to vote than those living in the capitol city, Amman.

Four arenas of authority are relevant to voting in Jordan: the state, tribe, family, and religion. With regard to the state, individuals are expected to vote for those who will represent their interests in the parliament. With regard to the tribe, parliamentary elections are an opportunity to respond to obligations, to demonstrate tribal allegiances, and, if one is lucky enough to have a tribal member elected, to activate the representative's obligations towards tribal members and secure access to resources. Tribal arenas thus promote voting for 'their own' as a way to seek and fulfil tribal obligations.[27] With regard to family, close-kin ties add an additional layer of obligation that goes beyond that of tribe, and one that is activated for Jordanians who do not identify with a tribe.[28] Finally, with regard to religion, Islamist communities promote voting for Islamist candidates as a demonstration of religious conviction.

Perhaps surprisingly, the state plays little direct role in Jordanians' choices over candidates. Jordanians generally do not see casting ballots as a way to ensure effective political change. Since the parliament's reopening in 1989, the legislative body has been increasingly impotent in the face of the monarchy, and citizens' trust in it has only declined (from 46 per cent of Jordanians stating they had some or great trust in the parliament in 2010 to only 14 per cent stating this in 2018) (Arab Barometer, 2019, pp. 8–9). Even most elites do not view obligations to the state as a primary reason to vote. An elite survey published in 2012 found only 30 per cent of 185 respondents said they participated in the 2010 elections because it was their national duty do so or in order to enhance democracy – compared to over half who said they did so due to their tribal or social ties (Al-Azzam, 2012, p. 355). Moreover, Jordanians may rely on the state for many things, but they do not need to vote to receive services in exchange. Electoral rules affect the choices before Jordanians, as we will see in Section 6, but obligations to the state and the expectations of rewards in the state arena do not drive voting.

Tribal, family, and religious arenas have greater influence on voters' decisions. For Jordanians of tribal origin, and particularly those living in rural areas, shaykhs play an important role in everyday life: they resolve disputes and help access services. At election time, many tribes use primaries to choose candidates and issue endorsements, sending clear messages that voters should

---

[27] It is not the point of the discussion here, but it is nevertheless worth noting that the return of competitive elections may strengthen tribalism by increasing the stakes associated with acting in accordance with social institutions in this arena of authority. There is evidence that multiparty elections reinforced tribalism not only in Jordan (Lust-Okar, 2009; Watkins, 2014), but also in Malawi (Englund, 2002; Kamwendo, 2002), Lebanon (Baylouny, 2010), and Zambia (Gadjanova, 2017).

[28] Jordanians of East Bank origin and those of Palestinian origin both have citizenship, but East Bank Jordanians generally have stronger tribal arenas of authority than Palestinians.

support 'their own' (Kao, 2015; Watkins, 2014). Obligations around family are even more strongly held. Even Jordanians of East Bank origin, for whom tribe is important, seek to have close relatives and family members elected over other tribal members, and some tribes institute rotation agreements that allow each family to take a turn accessing parliament. Finally, Jordanians rely on their religious community for spiritual guidance and well-being as well as financial and material support (Clark, 2004; Wiktorowicz, 2003). Thus, calls to support Islamist candidates have sway.

The extent to which these arenas influence electoral engagement depends on the electoral context and voters' characteristics. I find evidence of this in an analysis of survey data collected with Lindsay Benstead and Kristen Kao in 2014 (see Appendix B for details). Members of tribes were more likely to feel obligated to support and vote for a candidate who is a tribal or family member. This was especially true of those with little education and those living in rural areas, who are more highly dependent on tribes for governance and welfare. Moreover, when a change in the electoral law (described in Section 6) forced voters to choose between supporting candidates on the basis of religion or tribe, most rural Jordanians of East Bank origin supported their tribal candidate (see Patel, 2015). In contrast, those living in cities, where tribal influence over governance is weaker, were more likely to vote for a candidate supported by their local religious leader.

Or, to put this in a more stylized fashion, consider a Jordanian voter who has three candidates before her: a State Candidate, who is a non-Islamist, loyalist to the regime with no tribal or family ties to the candidate; a Tribal Candidate, who is a pious member of the voter's tribe but not her family; and an Islamist Candidate, who is a pious candidate but a vocal opponent of the monarchy. Note that the rules for the tribal and religious arenas are congruent if the candidate is both tribal and religious. If the voter makes choices based only on the state arena, they vote for the State Candidate, if only on the tribal arena, for the Tribal Candidate, and if on the religious arena, for the Islamist Candidate. In this example, taking the strength of the arena into account, they vote for the Tribal Candidate in rural areas and the Islamist Candidate in urban areas.

A perspective that pays attention to the strength of competing arenas of authority also helps explain variation in turnout. Voting is higher in rural areas, where tribal arenas are stronger. Voting is not purely voluntary, as tribal members sit outside polling stations to mark who has voted, sending out for those who fail to arrive.[29] Nor do all tribal members benefit in the future.

---

[29] Personal observation, 2010 and 2013 elections. Cammett (2014, pp. 63–4) notes that families do the same at polling stations in Lebanon.

Table 4 Arenas of authority, social institutions, and voting in Jordan

Arena of Authority	Relevant Social Institutions	Prescribed Choice	Strength of the Arena	
			Urban	Rural
State	Vote as a civic duty in order to uphold the state (and monarchy)	State Candidate	Low	Low
Tribal	Vote for co-tribal candidate in order to maintain or enhance status of the tribe; act reciprocally towards co-tribals	Tribal Candidate	Low	High
Religious	Vote for pious/ Islamist candidates in order to strengthen or uphold religious community/ensure Jordanians' religious morality	Islamist Candidate	Medium	Medium

In 2013, Jordanian women, gathering under a tent near a polling station in Tafilah, where they had been bussed in to rally for their tribal candidate, complained that the candidate would 'throw away his telephone' as soon as the elections were over.[30] Nevertheless, individuals vote, and they do so in response to the salience and strength the tribal arena has in elections. This explains why turnout in Jordan's 2013 elections reached nearly 80 per cent in rural tribal areas compared to 34 per cent in Amman.[31]

5 Social Institutions, Politics, and Development Outcomes

In this section, I turn to social institutions. As seen in Section 4, individuals' choices are influenced not only by the strength of competing arenas but also the nature of their institutions. The details of these institutions vary. Some prohibit engagement in 'earthly elections', denounce vaccinations, breastfeeding, or

---

[30] Author's fieldnotes.
[31] Turnout figures from Ministry of Interior website: MOI.GOV.JO (Arabic).

other practices often promoted by public health agencies, or require members to attend gender-segregated schools; others demand just the opposite. These have important implications for behaviour and outcomes, and scholars and practitioners should take them into account in research and development programming. Yet, such disparate rules also require an analytical structure for scholars and practitioners to make sense of them. Consequently, I build the framework around how different *types* of rules affect individuals' behaviour. I argue that rules governing group membership and boundaries, engagement, and roles are the basis for a tri-fold framework for constructing hypotheses and guiding future research, and I propose hypotheses for future consideration.

5.1 Group Membership and Boundary Maintenance Rules

As discussed in Section 3, arenas may have more or less porous borders, making it easier or more difficult for individuals to enter or exit the community. Boundary maintenance rules also establish how an individual should act in order to demonstrate allegiance to the community. This can be over appearance – the side curls of Hasidic Jewish men, the distinctive blue dresses and white bonnets of Amish women – or over actions, such a prohibitions against publicly airing views that oppose the group's tenets. Rules governing group membership and boundary maintenance not only help to establish and signify membership in the group, but also influence a wide range of engagement and outcomes, from electoral competition and representation to citizenship and policymaking.

Where boundaries are relatively closed, competition and participation take on new meaning. Campaign events become theatres for reinforcing community solidarity. People attend rallies because they want to show their support for and strengthen ties with the candidate and community; many are family, friends, neighbours, or co-congregationalists.[32] Events are technically public, but they border on exclusivity. This is particularly true in constituencies with competing, tightly knit communities. In a campaign study I conducted during the 2010 Jordanian elections, for instance, one researcher was asked to leave a campaign tent because he was from another local family and thus suspected of being a spy. The candidate and his entourage did not believe the event could be used to sway the man's vote. Similarly, surveys of individuals attending the Jordanian and Egyptian 2010 campaigns found that a large percentage of respondents saw

---

[32] A survey of campaign event attendees that I conducted during the 2010–11 Egyptian elections found that 40 per cent of respondents (n = 977) had a personal relationship with one of the candidates in the district. Nearly 45 per cent of attendees said the candidate had attended 'a dinner, funeral, wedding, Iftar or any other event at your house, or that of a family member in the past year', and about 43 per cent of attendees had received personal help from the candidate.

campaign events as 'closed'.[33] Even in Tunisia's 2011 campaign, which took place after the fall of Ben Ali and when public mobilization was especially high, 14 per cent of campaign attendees we surveyed viewed campaign events as exclusive.[34] In such cases the locus of competition shifts to the nomination stage (much as it does in one-party states). Tribes, families, and religious congregations choose candidates.[35] At times, they institute rules such as rotation of candidates across clans or families to reduce the potential for internal conflict, or even establish tribal primaries which are sometimes as formalized and hotly contested as general elections. Overall, the intention is to appear as a unified block, signalling to candidates outside the group that they are unlikely to succeed in garnering their votes.

A similar example is found in Libya. In 2012, a General National Congress (GNC) member described to me how rules aimed at maintaining the appearance of group coherence – or group boundary maintenance associated with the tribal arena – impacted elections. His small tribe had formed a coalition with two other tribes to run for a proportional representation (PR) seat in his district. They chose their coalition strategy by 'counting heads' of the different tribes, and they organized their campaign at weddings – a space in which their gatherings would be isolated from, and go undetected by, larger tribes that may have tried to undermine their efforts. Importantly, they knew that not every tribal member would support the selected candidate, but they nonetheless sought to maintain the appearance of cohesion. Fellow members could choose to not vote for their candidate, but to voice this intention publicly – and especially in favour of a candidate from another tribe – was unacceptable.[36] Such restrictions not only affect the outcome of elections, but also the expectations of other voters and the

---

[33] In Egypt, a public intercept survey conducted during the 2010 election campaigns found that nearly 69 per cent (n = 977) of individuals surveyed while they attended a campaign event said that they believed campaign events were open to all, 28 per cent said they were not, and 4 per cent did know answer; while of those surveyed through public intercept outside the events (about half of whom had attended an event previously), 53 per cent said that the events were open to all, 39 per cent believed they were not, and 8 per cent did not know. A smaller public intercept survey of 180 non-attendees in Jordan found that one-third of those surveyed felt the events were not open to all. See Appendix C for details.

[34] The survey included 585 attendees at campaign events in October 2011. See Appendix C for details.

[35] For instance, an elite survey conducted in Jordan found that candidates enter the race at the encouragement of family, friends, and the tribe. Interviews that a team of Jordanian researchers conducted with sixty candidates and campaign managers during the 2010 elections also found that candidates often began their campaigns after contacting, or being contacted by, family members (Lust et al., 2011, p. 121). For discussion of the use of mosques to mobilize support in Tunisia, see Belaam (2012).

[36] Author's interview with a GNC member participating in a Party Training Session, Tripoli, Libya (2012).

competitiveness of campaigns. When no one stands up in dissent, it is easier to believe everyone is united behind the candidate.

Boundary rules also play a role in the integration of refugees. Take, for instance, Jordanians' responses to refugees fleeing the Syrian civil war. In some cases, they treated refugees as outsiders whose presence they resented, but elsewhere, they admitted them into the community. In part, this was because boundary rules of tribal arenas of authority already designated them as part of the in-group. For instance, members of the Bani Khalid tribe, which spans Jordan, Lebanon, and Syria, were 'welcomed and accepted into the Jordanian community because they carried the same tribal name' (Miettunen and Shunnaq, 2020, p. 11). They were integrated, at least in part, because they entered the community as a member of the same tribal arena – one which transcended state borders.

Boundary rules governing social arenas of authority affect relations with the state as well. Lauren MacLean (2010) shows how group boundary rules of the Akan in Ghana and Cote d'Ivoire shaped individuals' relationships with the state. In Ghana, boundary rules designated a wider range of individuals as community members, but the rules governing members' commitments only required low levels of mutual support. In contrast, in Cote d'Ivoire, boundary rules restricted community entry to a close circle of family members, but required they provide each other a higher level of assistance. She argues that this had important implications for how individuals engaged with the state. Ghanaians had a much closer relationship with the state, viewed local officials as key actors, and saw engagement with the state in terms of *civic duty*, while Ivoirians understood the state to be a remote entity, and any interaction with it as the reserve of '*big men*'.

Finally, studies of mobilization around AIDS issues also demonstrate the importance of group boundaries on political engagement and policymaking. Cathy Cohen's (1999) study of the African American community's response to AIDS found that the community initially viewed the epidemic as one afflicting gay, white men, and, for some in the community, God's punishment for sinful activity. Consequently, the leadership shied away from pressing for responsive policies. Similarly, Evan Lieberman's (2009) study of AIDS policies in Africa found that where group boundaries are strong (i.e., less porous), there was less support for broad policy responses to the epidemic. Where the disease came to be associated with certain groups – as in South Africa, where whites saw it as a 'black disease', while blacks perceived it as a 'white disease' – the policy discussion was one of blame and stigmatization, with little support for broad-based policies.

In short, boundary rules influence individuals' behaviour and, ultimately, policymaking and development outcomes. The extant literature suggests some hypotheses that require further investigation. Stronger, less porous boundaries appear linked to more encompassing prescriptions on the behaviours of members, the appearance of less competition, and more difficulty for elites in other arenas to try to mobilize members across boundaries. This can have implications for policymaking and implementation when issues are associated with certain communities. Where there are less porous boundaries, in-group members may express greater support for policy responses, but they may be less willing and able to reach across boundaries to other communities, and thus to gain their support.

5.2 Rules of Engagement: Individualism-Collectivism

A second set of rules revolve around engagement: who is expected to act, how, and with regard to what? Here, I focus on the distinction between rules of engagement based in individualism and those centred on collectivism, a distinction that Harry Triandis (2001, p. 907) has called the single-most important cultural distinction.[37] This distinction has significant implications for the likelihood that individuals contribute to public goods or participate in political action, and, consequently, welfare and development outcomes.

All social institutions govern communities and are, in that sense, communal, but they differ in the extent to which they frame action in terms of individual or collective goals. In individualism, social institutions aim to create and maintain a community in which individuals are autonomous and encouraged to self-actualize. In collectivism, individuals' independent desires are subordinate to the collective, and the 'good' is determined by what benefits the collective, not the individual (see Markus and Kitayama, 1991; Triandis, 1989). Those transgressing a community norm – speaking out against established power, voting for an 'unacceptable' candidate, refusing to contribute to community initiatives – bring not only social shame or physical and material harm to themselves, but also to others in the community. So, too, those who improve their welfare raise the community's status and benefit all.

Whether social institutions centre on individualism or collectivism influences individuals' decisions to contribute to community development.[38] The traditional

---

[37] The individualism-collectivism distinction is long recognized in anthropology, psychology, and sociology. It is akin to what Talcott Parsons and Edward Shils in *Toward a General Theory of Action* (1951) referred to as self-orientation versus collectivity orientation, and what Geert Hofstede (1982) later saw as individualism-collectivism.

[38] There are important questions to be asked about how the conditions under which the willingness to contribute to local community actions, and expectations of responsiveness to one's group, affects economic growth and governance. Some studies find a link between a society's orientation on the communalism-individualism dimension at the national level and economic development (for a review, see Ball, 2001). However, as Ball (2001) argues, whether collectivism promotes or impedes economic development depends at least in part on the size of the community.

statement of the collective action problem presumes individualism. Individuals want to benefit from the collective good, so if their own actions alone will not determine success and if they will benefit regardless of their own actions, they will choose not to contribute. They need selective incentives, or to be engaged in an iterated game (Axelrod, 1984), in order to do otherwise. In contrast, in collectivism, the same conditions apply: individuals' actions alone will not determine success and they may benefit from success regardless of their contribution. But collectivism entails additional incentives to contribute. Identifying one's self with the community or holding strong notions of solidarity may drive contributions (e.g., Lawler, 1992). It is not surprising, thus, that social movements often put forth frames intended to inculcate collectivism (Benford and Snow, 2000). Moreover, where social institutions require one to put the collective good above one's own, failing to do so may incur sanctions. Collectivism is not to be equated with 'warm and fuzzy' feelings (Liu et al., 2019). In-group vigilance and social sanctions associated with collectivism can be painful, particularly where networks are strong (Hu et al., 2015).

Studying Ghanaian villages and their home town associations in the Netherlands, Mazzucato and Kabki (2009) show how collectivist social institutions foster community contributions. They describe institutions that local villages designed to ensure funeral contributions. Funerals are perhaps the most important of ceremonies in Ghana, and holding a funeral in one's hometown is an act that both represents belonging and affords an opportunity to fundraise for the bereaved, maintaining social insurance. In these villages, funerals are also an opportunity to collect funds for the village, as 10 per cent of the contributions go to village development funds and 90 per cent to the bereaved family. Importantly, traditional authorities require their subjects to contribute to these funds regardless of whether they are residing in the village or abroad, attending the funeral or not. Moreover, according to the social institutions described, failure to pay incurs collective punishment: a family is not allowed to hold a funeral anywhere on the village's territory if past funeral dues are unpaid. Migrants' families back home are shamed if they fail to pay, and migrants suffer the costs of this shame. Thus, diaspora's contributions to funeral costs and other collective causes, which are critical to development outcomes, continue in part because family members back home constitute linkages with collectivist social institutions. Importantly, Mazzucato and Kabki (2009) note that such institutions are effective in small villages, where monitoring and enforcement are easier (i.e., local arenas are stronger).

Whether social institutions are individualist or collectivist also shapes political participation. Indeed, distinguishing between individualism and collectivism may help reconcile debates found in the literature on clientelism and voting. Many studies of vote-buying assume that voters act within individualist contexts, and vote-buying is a one-shot exchange between a broker and voter. Scholars then ask how brokers and candidates ensure that voters support them after the handouts are given. They search for mechanisms that facilitate monitoring (Stokes, 2005; see also Hicken and Nathan, 2020 for a review), or less frequently, individual-level traits – such as a strong intrinsic sense of reciprocity – that explain why voters remain true to brokers (Finan and Schechter, 2012; Lawson and Greene, 2014).

Yet, a very different picture emerges if collectivist social institutions drive voters' decisions. Citizens may support candidates who are members of their community (e.g., family or kin, coethnic, or from the same locality) at least in part because they feel duty-bound to do so (Cruz, 2019; Kao, 2015; Ravanilla et al., 2021; Schaffer, 1998; 2014). They may also believe candidates from their community are equally duty-bound to help them meet their everyday needs, easing their way through a maze of sluggish, unresponsive bureaucracy (Lust-Okar, 2006; 2009). Voters thus support the candidate because they believe that the candidate they support is the one who is obligated to help them or their community, given collectivist institutions in arenas of authority outside the state. As one Jordanian put it, 'Everyone in [Jordan] needs a VIP to solve his problems' (Lust et al., 2011, p. 120). The question for scholars and practitioners, then, is not which version of clientelism is correct but rather which social institutions structure individuals' choices, and thus, what assumptions should guide research and programming.

In sum, the individualist-collectivist distinction in social institutions appears to have important implications. Where social institutions are individualist, one can expect contributions are made along the logic of the collective action problem and selective incentives may be required to motivate contributions. However, where institutions are collectivist, selective incentives are likely to be less effective. Social sanctions meted out by the community when individuals place their interests over those of the community motivate compliance. In short, much as state institutions that promote patriotism can engender individuals' sacrifice for sake of the community, social institutions based on collectivism can spur cooperation.

5.3 Rules Governing Roles: Leadership Selection and Tenure

The final set of rules regard the roles individuals hold. In this section, I focus on rules governing leadership selection and tenure. These influence the extent to which leaders have influence over other community members, and the ability of community members to hold leaders accountable.

Leadership selection rules determine who is eligible to rule and who has a voice in choosing the leader, what Bruce Bueno de Mesquita and his colleagues called the 'selectorate' (Bueno de Mesquita et al., 2003). These determine the level of competition, ranging from highly competitive contexts, where many are eligible for leadership and the selectorate is large, to less competetive environments, in which the number of contenders is small and the selectorate limited.

There is widespread evidence that leaders are more responsive to members when the level of competition over leadership is higher. Chieftaincies in Sierra Leonne are found to be less repressive and yield better development outcomes when leadership selection is more competitive (Acemoglu et al., 2014). A similar association exists between higher competition and better public goods provision in the Philippines (Cruz et al., 2020). So too, Jordanians enjoy better municipal services where there is greater competition over local elections (Gao, 2016), while in India, slum dwellers benefit when party brokers compete with each other (Auerbach, 2019).

Leaders, like others, are members of multiple arenas of authority, and the extent to which they respond to demands made by those in different arenas depends, in part, on how critical these arenas are to their success. Consider, for instance, Lebanese politicians, who act as elites in both sectarian communities and political parties, as well as within their respective arenas of authority. Melani Cammett (2014) finds that service providers connected to sectarian-based political parties in Lebanon favour in-group members in districts where their sect is large enough to win elections, but that they do not do so in districts in which voters from their sect do not constitute the plurality. In deciding to *whom* they grant favour, these politicians respond to demands from their party (and competition for leadership within it) and demands from their sect. Their decision to serve outsiders, which can be understood as the fulfilment, or not, of obligations to favour their sectarian community, is based on the logic of political competition.

Rules over the length of leadership tenure affect leader responsiveness as well. When leaders' tenure is long and their welfare dependent on the community (e.g., exit options are limited), they can personally benefit from the development of their local area. Drawing on Mancur Olson's (1993) concept of a stationary bandit, Kate Baldwin (2016) argues that leaders with longer time horizons are more likely to see the benefits of fostering development. Thus, traditional authorities in Zambia act as development brokers, and not simply vote brokers, because the traditional institution of life-long hereditary rule encourages them to invest in their area's development.

Yet, to be a 'stationary bandit' requires that the leader enjoys security. Jeffrey Paller's (2019, p. 20) study of urban politics in Ghana points to how land security influences leader responsiveness. He distinguishes between three types of settlements: indigenous settlements (with leaders most akin to Baldwin's stationary bandits), stranger settlements (with diverse communities but secure land tenure), and squatter settlements (newly emerging settlements with no sense of belonging and little land security). In the latter, he argues, leaders do not face periodic elections or other term limits, but they focus more on their position within other communities (and arenas of authority) than on the local settlement. He explains:

> [a]lthough [squatter settlements] have strong and active leaders, they are motivated by a personal agenda to accumulate power and support a constituency elsewhere, usually in the home region from which they migrated. Therefore, distributive politics follows a private logic, where leaders capture state resources for personal gain.[39]

In short, the rules that govern leader selection and removal are likely to affect leaders' responsiveness to members' demands and, consequently, politics and development outcomes. Leaders are more likely to be responsive when they are chosen from members in the immediate arena of authority, when they expect to have a long tenure, and when their welfare is closely tied to that of the community. In this way, expectations again mirror many of those found regarding the state: states with more democratic, stable regimes are expected to be responsive, fostering economic growth and human development.

5.4 Illustration: Social Institutions, Land Titling, and Property Rights

To illustrate the insights from bringing arenas of authority and social institutions into analyses of politics and development, I return to the issue of state land titling. Recall from Section 3 that less than one-third of the global population had state-backed property titles in 2017, despite strong efforts to institute state land titles. Considering how assumptions underlying land titling do, or do not, comport with the lived experiences of land users thus sheds light on the barriers to titling and encourages thinking about alternative ways to enhance land security.

Efforts to advance state land titling are based on several fundamental assumptions. As John Bruce and Shem Migot-Adholla (1994, p. 3) note, the notion that

---

[39] Even leaders who have shorter time horizons and may not always invest in development may choose to do so when the issue is urgent or affects them in the short run. There may be some instances in which less competition results in better service provision. van der Windt and Voors (2020) argue that stronger chiefs more effectively combated Ebola in Sierra Leone. This raises important questions regarding the conditions under which performance may depend on the issue area.

land tenure security is 'the perceived right by the possessor of a land parcel to manage and use the parcel, dispose of its produce and engage in transactions, including temporary or permanent transfers, without hindrance or interference from any person or corporate entity' is critical to both land registration and titling. In accordance with the state-centric approaches discussed in Section 2, the state is portrayed as the dominant, or at least potentially dominant, arena of authority, and an impartial actor – the protector of land users' rights. Moreover, land users are expected to enjoy easy entry and exit into geographical communities and thus to be able to access land or dispose of it at will; and the rules of engagement are individualistic, allowing users to make decisions independent of community goals and considerations.

Yet, the state is often not the most salient arena for individuals seeking access to land. For many in the world, the state is a distant actor, largely absent from their lives, and when present, often not trusted.[40] Local traditional leaders and other community members, in contrast, are very much present and more often trusted. They are the key to solving disputes, receiving social assistance, accessing services, and – importantly – securing land (Logan, 2013). Moreover, as we show in Malawi and Zambia, local traditional authorities are often more likely than the state to monitor and sanction non-compliers (Baldwin et al., 2021). Not surprisingly, in a study aimed at understanding the value of localizing state administrative services, Boniface Dulani, Hannah Swilah, and I (2016, p. 12) found that Malawians preferred titles from their local chiefs over state titles because, they argued, their property is insecure without chiefs' support. Their remarks echoed the cautions from Bruce and Migot-Adholla (1994, p. 8): 'a formal title certificate or other official document is, at best, merely an affirmation of this social guarantee; it does not create it'.

It is not just the relative strength of the state vis-à-vis customary arenas of authority that limits the advance of state titling, but also the disconnect between assumptions underlying state titling projects and the nature of social institutions that govern individuals' experiences around land. In much of the world, communities are governed by collectivist institutions, and land is an important component of community identity. Access to land is understood as part of one's right as a member of the community, as determined by ancestry and belonging. Individuals from outside the community do not have the right to simply acquire it, or those from inside the community to dispose of land as they wish. Outsiders may obtain land, but the community can, and does, expel them from the area if land pressures rise (Berge et al., 2014; Takane, 2008). That is,

---

[40] The LGPI survey (Lust et al., 2019) found that 12 per cent of respondents in the Zambian border region were worried their land may be taken, and of these, nearly half (41 per cent) worried it would be taken by the state. See Appendix C for details.

the boundaries to the local arena of authority are often largely impermeable, and collectivist institutions limit the ability of individuals to transfer property as they wish. Moreover, as Adam Harris and Lauren Honig (2022) show, many Malawians and Zambians have higher trust in neighbours who rely on customary land tenure, and they anticipate greater cooperation from them as well. The individualist underpinnings of state land titling are often at odds with the social institutions in the dominant, local arenas of authority.

This is not to say that concerns about land security are misplaced. Systems governing land rights outside the state often create insecurity, particularly for some groups. As noted earlier, outsiders often face greater land insecurity, as the community can invoke rules over boundaries at any time. Lineage-based inheritance laws and residence patterns disadvantage men or women, depending on whether they are matrilineal or patrilineal, respectively (Berge et al., 2014; Kutsoati and Morck, 2016). But such insecurity and inequalities also exist with regard to the state. The 2019 LGPI survey reveals that 15 per cent of Malawians and 12 per cent of Zambians in the border region were worried that they may lose access to their land. Importantly, they see a range of threats, from relatives and customary leaders to commercial farmers, as well as the state.[41] Understanding which arenas of authority are most salient, and the institutions governing them, is key to determining which groups are most at risk.

Solutions to land security problems thus need to take into account how individuals experience the relative strength of different arenas of authority, and the social institutions within them. One approach is to formalize customary land tenure arrangements. In Malawi, Karen Ferree, Lauren Honig, Melanie Phillips, and I (2022) find that individuals prefer land with written documents regardless of whether they are offered by the state or a chief, and they do so as much to signal to other citizens in their community that they hold the land as to benefit from state-backed security. This is not surprising, given the fear many have that other community members may try to grab their land. Another option, for those who seek to strengthen the state, is to design solutions that incorporate social institutions. For instance, Berge and colleagues (2014) point to Norway's *odel* system as an example of how customary lineage rights can be incorporated into state law. The *odel*, which has been around for thousands of years, gives first rights of purchase to those in the kinship circle who have controlled the land for a fixed period. Incorporating such a system into a state titling scheme does

---

[41] More specifically, of the 15% who feared losing land in the Malawian border region, 46% most feared their relatives, 6% feared the state, 29% feared customary leaders, and 1% saw commercial farmers as the threat. In Zambia, of the 12% who expressed feelings of land insecurity, 6% feared relatives, 41% feared the state, 28% feared customary leaders, and 1% feared commercial farmers.

not overcome the weakness of the state, but it can make state law compatible with social institutions.

6 Reconsidering 'State' Institutions

A perspective that overlooks competing arenas of authority and associated social institutions not only fails to understand how these forces affect politics and development, but also to make sense of state institutions. Electoral engagement, contributions to community development projects, and public service provision have multiple meanings. They are not only opportunities to choose lawmakers, fill coffers, or provide services, but also to uphold obligations as members of ethnic, religious, geographic, or other arenas of authority. In negotiating over institutions associated with the state, elites are often also negotiating over institutions that will shape individuals' incentives and actions pertaining to social institutions in arenas of authority outside of the state. These insitutions affect the the extent to which social obligations are upheld and may strengthen, maintain, or undermine elites' authority within those arenas. Consequently, arenas of authority and social institutions not only influence how individuals navigate established institutions, but also shape preferences over, and therefore the designs of, state institutions.

In this section, I demonstrate how arenas of authority and social institutions shape preferences over, and ultimately the nature of, electoral rules, administrative boundaries, and political parties – three sets of institutions that scholars and practitioners often associate exclusively with the state. In doing so, I draw into question the cordoning off of 'state' institutions from other arenas of authority. Just as actions have multiple meanings, so do institutions. Electoral rules, administrative boundaries, and political parties are institutions both within and outside the state, at one and the same time.

6.1 Electoral Rules

Electoral rules are conventionally viewed as political institutions that influence engagement and representation. They are the outcomes of negotiations in which political actors are centre stage. Taking this approach, for instance, Boix (1999) argues that the relative size of political parties determines whether elites establish PR or majoritarian rules. Scholars and practitioners increasingly recognize that other forces play a role. Some note that electoral rules may not work as expected because context (e.g., social divisions and norms, weak rule of law and media systems, and electoral fraud and intimidation) mediates outcomes (Ferree et al., 2013; 2014; Krook and Moser, 2013), while others consider how electoral institutions activate fault lines, determining which identities are salient

(Chandra, 2007; Posner, 2005). These approaches are insightful but not fully sufficient. They explore how elites' negotiation of electoral rules shape elections but fall short of comprehending how the same considerations impact other arenas of authority. A more complete understanding is essential as academic perspectives influence praxis; political scientists not only study electoral rules, they also engineer them (Carey et al., 2013; Htun and Powell, 2013).

The story of the Libyan 2012 GNC electoral law illustrates how arenas of authority outside the state respond to electoral rules, and reciprocally shape electoral institutions and outcomes. The electoral law, formulated after the downfall of Muammar Qhaddafi, was the subject of extensive international intervention. Electoral engineers prepared plans based on their best understanding of Libya's conditions and electoral institutions. Yet, they failed to anticipate how elites in arenas of authority outside the state, intent on maintaining their communities' social institutions, would respond and ultimately upend the electoral engineers' best-laid plans.

The preferences of international experts and the larger political parties were constructed within the paradigm of elections as a state institution. International experts generally advocated a PR system with gender quotas; they believed these would strengthen political parties, which were nearly absent in the wake of the previous regime,[42] and promote the status of women in a society where most held conservative views on gender roles.[43] Many elites returning from abroad (with few domestic bases of support) and the Muslim Brotherhood (the largest party) favoured a PR system with gender quotas for the same reasons. Given the nascent state of parties in Libya, however, the proposal was a two-tiered, mixed electoral system, with PR seats evenly distributed across the country in larger constituencies on one tier and majoritarian seats on a second tier.

However, local elites viewed electoral institutions not only as a state institution but also as one associated with other arenas of authority. Elites in parts of the country where boundaries around ethnic, tribal, or locality-based arenas of authority were strong – and where there were deep divisions between neighbouring villages – could not accept the possibility that a politician from a neighbouring area would be their representative. Moreover, social institutions within these arenas prohibited women from working outside the home or

---

[42] Qhaddafi not only had banned political parties but also made party membership a crime punishable by death. At the eve of the first Libyan elections, many citizens reported they feared political parties (Doherty, 2012).

[43] In 2014, nearly 69 per cent of Libyans agreed that 'When jobs are scarce, men should have more right to a job than women' (p. 85), and 75 per cent agreed or strongly agreed that 'On the whole, men make better political leaders than women do' (p. 97) (World Values Survey, 2018).

traveling without a male companion, yet alone going to Tripoli to represent their constituency. Consequently, these elites rejected the proposed system not only (or even primarily) because of its impact on electoral behaviour and representation but also because it would potentially, and fundamentally, undermine their arenas of authority and the social institutions within them.

Negotiations over districting and seat distribution regarding the division of proportional representation (list, or PR) and independent candidate (IC) seats ultimately resulted in a complicated, hybrid system – and one much different than the electoral engineers intended. As shown in Figure 1, areas such as Gheryan, where there were strong local leaders and distinct tribal identities, accepted only IC seats, and PR seats were redistributed to areas such as Tripoli, with a larger number of residents from other regions of the country and returnees from abroad. Altogether, fifty of the seventy districts had parallel voting (e.g., voting for both PR and IC seats), while nineteen districts had only IC seats and four districts only PR seats. Put simply, the result was a hodgepodge system that reflected compromises between elites aiming to accommodate demands emerging from different ethnic and local arenas of authority and the social institutions within them. The compromise averted conflicts (at the time) but also complicated election logistics and created inequalities in representation.[44]

In contrast, electoral engineers in Jordan devised rules that worked in concert with elites in both tribal arenas and the state, achieving both parties' desired outcomes. At the end of the 1980s, Jordan reinstated multiparty parliamentary elections and allowed political parties to mobilize. The goal was to reduce opposition around economic crises and ease Jordan's entry into a peace treaty with Israel. But the parliament elected in 1989 was a nuisance at best and destabilizing at worst. Parliamentarians frequently opposed government policy, with the Islamic Action Front (IAF) leading the opposition. Consequently, the monarchy changed the electoral law in 1993, aiming to weaken the opposition. The new electoral law moved from the 1989 electoral law's multi-member district (MMD)/multi-vote system to an MMD/single, non-transferable vote (SNTV) one.

The result was what both the state and tribal elites wanted: a significant weakening of the Islamists and reinforcement of tribal arenas of authority. Individuals previously could divide their votes, casting one vote for their tribal leader and a second vote for the candidate who represented their policy preferences. After 1993, they were limited to one vote. When required to choose between casting votes in response to social institutions in tribal arenas of

---

[44] I discussed the gap between the intent and effect of the electoral design in 2012 with key stakeholders when I was part of a consulting team that implemented surveys and provided political parties with information on citizens' concerns. The disconnect between intent and outcome is also reflected in The Carter Center (2012b, pp. 18–25).

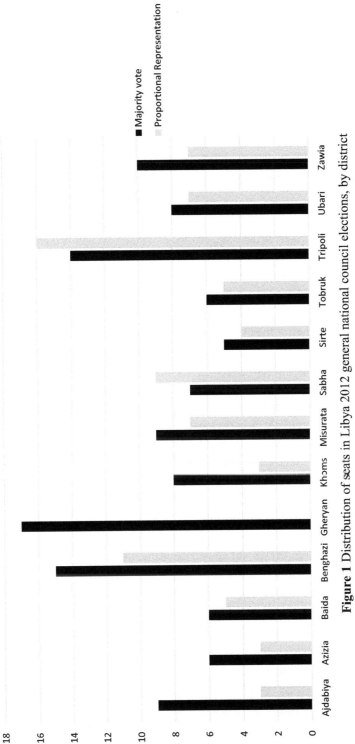

Figure 1 Distribution of seats in Libya 2012 general national council elections, by district

Source: The Carter Center, 2012b, Appendix G.

authority and those in religious ones, most East Bank Jordanians supported their tribal authorities (recall reasons for this described in Section 4). Thus, Islamists (not all of whom were IAF) saw their share of Jordan's eighty legislative seats fall from thirty-four seats in 1989 to twenty-two seats in the 1993 (Schwedler, 2015). Islamists' presence in parliament was further reduced through their boycott of the 1997 and 2010 elections. In contrast, seventy-five independents gained seats in the 1997 elections, including sixty-eight tribal chiefs (Inter-Parliamentary Union, 1997), and more than ninety tribes were represented after 2010 (Hanandah, 2010). The electoral rule's alignment with tribal social institutions produced these outcomes.[45]

6.2 Administrative Boundary-Drawing

Arenas of authority outside the state, and social institutions within them, affect the development of administrative boundaries as well. Administrative boundaries are often drawn along tribal or sectarian lines, as a response to demands from social groups. When this fails to be the case, they are often the subject of contestation.

Grossman and Lewis (2014) find this in Uganda. They argue that ethnic groups in outlying areas of their district seek territorial secession when they are of a different group than the majority of those in the district centre. This is because these groups perceive themselves to be disadvantaged by the district centre and thus demand a district to gain greater spoils. Importantly, however, the disadvantage comes not from the logic of the state system but rather because resources are demanded and believed to flow along ethnic lines. That is, the ethnic arenas, and social institutions regarding responsiveness to in-group members, drive resource distribution and, hence, the demand for new districts.

State bureaucrats can face strong resistance when they attempt to ignore these arenas. Tunisian bureaucrats attempting to draw municipal boundaries as part of the decentralization process in post-revolutionary Tunisia learned this first hand (Kherigi, 2021b). Mokhtar Hammami, the head of the Ministry of Interior's Department for Local Authorities (DGCPL) and bureaucrat who led the boundary-making process, took pride in the Ministry's formulaic, 'neutral' process – or, put differently, a process that privileged the state. He explained:

---

[45] Implementation of the gender quota in Jordan similarly reflects the influence of social institutions. The quota set aside seats for the women who gained the largest percentages of votes in their districts. Given gerrymandering that has led to small, rural districts (largely centred around tribes) and larger urban districts, it was far easier for women to gain seats in rural areas than urban ones. Moreover, minority tribes ran women in these districts as a strategy to gain a tribal seat. The result was that rural woman tended to fill the quota seats, many of whom had very conservative positions on gender issues. See Bush and Gao (2017).

When we did all this work – the sociological aspect, we did not take it seriously. … We need sociologists by our side to study it, is this tribe or group there compatible with that one. … We could not get into these discussions. … It's not necessary; that was our position because we were working on things that were [pause] neutral. That was our goal. … Sometimes there are two clans that … want to be integrated in one imeda. … But if we get into this issue, we will never get out of it. (Kherigi, 2021a, pp. 21–2)

The result, however, was that local communities contested the new boundaries. Like the Libyans described earlier, Tunisians living in areas where arenas based on local ties were strong were unwilling to be either joined with 'strangers' in the municipality or split from relatives by municipal boundaries. Local elites fought to ensure that state boundaries were consistent with, and reinforced, social institutions within their arenas of authority, and often they succeeded. Kherigi (2021b) reports that the Ministry of Local Affairs faced hundreds of complaints and was forced in many cases to modify the boundaries.

6.3 Political Parties

Arenas of authority and social institutions also affect the development of political parties and party systems. As with electoral rules, scholars and practitioners primarily view political parties and party systems in terms of the state as organizations and systems that structure competition over political office. These scholars recognize that social context influences the development of parties and party systems (Boix, 1997; Lipset and Rokkan, 1967), but do not explicitly consider arenas of authority and the social institutions within them. These authorities not only influence the development of parties and party systems, but also give them meaning that extends beyond their roles in the state.

Where the state is weak and other arenas of authority strong, there is little incentive to form political parties. Kuwait offers a striking example of how non-state arenas of authority can substitute for political parties. There, parties are illegal, although political 'tendencies' exist. More importantly, politically active elites appear satisfied with this arrangement. They rely instead on tribes and, to a lesser extent, business networks to hold gatherings (diwaniya) and debate political issues, to select electoral candidates, and to mobilize voters. Thus, although Kuwait has one of the most politically active and contentious societies in the Gulf, Kuwaitis have not rallied for the right to form political parties. However, when the Emir unexpectedly began to enforce a decade-old law prohibiting tribal primaries in 2008, Kuwaitis were enraged. Banning political parties was one thing, but eliminating tribal primaries completely unacceptable (Tetreault, 2014).

Jordan, too, illustrates how non-state arenas can undermine the development of political parties. Recall from the previous discussion that Jordan has strong kinship arenas of authority, with social institutions that require individuals to cast their ballots for co-tribal candidates. Tribes, then, often act as political parties – engaging in primaries and get-out-the-vote efforts. Even when they form political parties, often it is because, as one Jordanian tribal elite once told me, that's how modern politics is played. The result is what Mainwaring and Scully (1995) describe as inchoate party systems, where parties are dominated by individual personalities, have low organizational capacity, and develop shallow roots in society.

Political parties thus established are an example of isomorphism, the development of organizations that are political parties in form but not substance. They do not play by the textbook roles: to develop policy positions to represent their group interests, recruit and nominate candidates, or educate and mobilize the citizens. Instead, they act as organizations (at times subsidized by state coffers or international donors) that require and reward members of non-state arenas of authority for demonstrating their allegiance. They are instruments of social arenas as well as the state.

This affects how citizens engage with the parties, as well as how parties evolve. In Jordan, for instance, citizens spend little time during the campaign period seeking information about candidates or their positions. Detailed assessments of candidates' qualities and platforms are not necessary; they simply need to look at which candidate represents their community. Consequently, fragmentation has persisted. Jordanian candidates have won seats with as little as 2 per cent of the popular vote, the margin of votes between last winner and first loser is often in double digits, and the percentage of wasted votes reach as high as two-thirds of the total vote count; in the 2010 parliamentary elections, 12 seats (10 per cent of the total) saw fewer than 100 votes separating winners and losers. Such results leave would-be candidates in upcoming elections sufficient reason to believe they have a chance of winning, even with relatively few resources (National Democratic Institute, 2010, p. 36). Large numbers of candidates and low margins of victory thus both result from and promote high turnover in parliamentary seats. Not surprisingly, in 2010, Jordan saw nearly two-thirds turnover in parliamentary seats, and in 2007, three-fourths of the representatives entered for the first time (Lust et al., 2011, p. 127).

6.4 Implication: The Role and Development of (Non-)State Institutions

Electoral rules, administrative boundaries, and political parties are often viewed as state-based institutions; yet, as the aforementioned examples illustrate, they often are both shaped by and act as institutions in arenas outside the state. Electoral rules, for instance, can affect the extent to which individuals have incentives to demonstrate their allegiance to their tribe, locality, or other social group. Gender quotas can alter the rewards associated with following obligations for women to stay removed from the public sphere. So, too, actors and organizations associated with non-state arenas can act as substitutes for institutions associated with the state. The ability of tribal, religious, or other organizations to coordinate candidates and mobilize support undermines party development, but it also means that one finds the relevant institutions that shape electoral mobilization in tribes or other arenas, not in the state. Institutions associated with the state are often institutions of non-state arenas as well, and institutions in non-state arenas often shape engagement in the state. That is, institutions are not always either state or non-state institutions but may act in multiple arenas of authority at the same time.

This has important implications for development practitioners and policymakers. Consider democracy promotion, for instance. Political party subsidies may have little impact on competition if the institutions that mobilize support and shape representation are found in other institutions. So, too, trainings that focus on campaign messaging will have very little impact if voters make their decisions based on whether a candidate is from their community, rather than the policies they espouse. Finally, as the example from Libya shows all too well, electoral rules that are designed without taking into account how these rules are both state and non-state institutions can have unintended consequences. Actors intent on state-building need to consider how institutions can be simultaneously institutions of state and non-state arenas.

7 Conclusion

The dominant perspective on governance and development has privileged the state. Definitionally, scholars and practitioners often ascribe the state dominance over all other social organizations. Intellectually, scholars under-theorize non-state authorities and institutions. Practically, they devise programmes that seek to improve human welfare by shaping primarily state political and administrative institutions.

Yet, there is a disconnect between this perspective and how people act in practice. The functions typically associated with the state (e.g., security, public goods provision) are in fact not *state* imperatives but essentials for any organized society. Moreover, individuals are not only citizens, but also members of other communities within non-state arenas of authority, located within or spanning across state boundaries, which also aim to fulfil these functions.

And within these, social institutions (e.g., roles, rules, and associated rewards) shape their actions and, ultimately, development outcomes. Individuals thus navigate competing arenas – of which the state is but one. Scholars, practitioners, and policymakers need to place the state and other arenas of authority on equal footing in theory building and development programming.

Doing so requires a common framework to draw findings together, guide future research, and design development programmes. A framework allows the recasting and reconciling of extant research. It provides a unified language and averts confusion created by the multiple meanings of key constructs such as 'social institutions'. It places in perspective approaches that focus on single arenas of authority (e.g., religion and politics, ethnicity) or discrete aspects of social institutions (e.g., networks, rules of reciprocity, or altruism). It calls for reconsidering underlying assumptions found, for instance, in studies of institutional strength (e.g., networks, social capital, and social density) that presume uniform rules of engagement, or in studies of rules (e.g., ethnicity and cooperation) that presume uniform institutional strength. A framework makes it possible to draw broader lessons from illuminating, but seemingly disparate, literatures on traditional authorities, ethnic identity, social networks, and other aspects of arenas of authority and social institutions. It fosters reflection on which how individuals perceive the meaning of the acts in which they engage, the rules that govern these choices, and the implications of their choices.

7.1 Defining Arenas and Social Institutions

Taking the competing arenas of authority and social institutions that affect individuals' decisions into account requires that they be well defined. These are not merely the residuals, defined by what is left over after one has taken the state and its institutions into account. Nor should they be understood only as disruption to the state – corruption, clientelism, or capture. Finally, they are not simply identity groups. Arenas may be based on ethnicity, religion, or other identities; however, it is not the nature of the identity but rather the characteristics of arenas and institutions that shape action. The goal is not just to recognize that ethnicity, religion, or other identities affect the choices made by voters and politicians, citizens, and service providers. It is to understand how differences in the nature of these arenas and institutions outside the state shape their engagement – regardless of the identity on which they are based.

Arenas of authority are spheres of engagement. They have a community which acts within its boundaries, distinguishing members from non-members outside. Unlike states, social arenas of authority need not be territorially bounded. However, individuals within arenas are bound together by a common goal to perpetuate the community. Individual members may have competing interests, but they are engaged in a common project. This requires governance over a range of actions, from how individuals enter or exit the community to what roles they may hold, and how they act with members and outsiders.

Social institutions delineate the roles, rules, and rewards that govern communities within the arena of authority. These determine who has power and how they maintain it, the actions that are permitted or prohibited, how adherence accords benefits and transgressions incur sanctions. Social institutions are not simply beliefs or practices (habits); in contrast to beliefs, they are rules about what one should and should not do, and unlike habits, they have an intentionality that is driven by anticipated costs and benefits. Nor are they social networks, social capital, social actors, or any of the other myriad 'socials' that are used, somewhat interchangeably, in the literature.

Social institutions vary significantly both across arenas and across time. It may be easier or harder for individuals to enter or exit the arena (e.g., creating boundaries that are more porous or impermeable), or for individuals to change their roles or be selected as leaders (e.g., social mobility). Rules governing how individuals engage with others in the community – whether women and men can debate issues together, whether youth can challenge their elders, whether in-group members can police inter- and intra-group conflicts – differ in important ways, even across arenas formed around the same identities.

7.2 Charting the Path Forward

A framework that takes arenas of authority and social institutions into account prompts analysts and practitioners to ask a number of questions: which arenas of authority matter for the issue at hand? How do the social institutions within the different arenas shape behaviour and development outcomes? (See Figure 2.) Moving forward requires fully interrogating expectations derived from the extant literature, answering new questions that emerge from the framework, and addressing methodological challenges.

7.2.1 Initial Expectations

The answer to the question of which arenas of authority are relevant to the issue at hand is less obvious than it may appear. Actions often have multiple meanings: voting for a candidate is an act of choosing a policy, but also a demonstration of allegiance to an ethnic group or adherence to a religious doctrine; deciding whether or not to doctor an injured rebel is a choice of allegiance to the state, but also of support for a local community or commitment to a professional oath. Not all arenas are relevant to all decisions, and they are not always in conflict. But to know when

Impact of State and Other Arenas of Authority

What are the implications of the choices at hand?

How do authorities view these actions and decisions?

How do individuals view the relevant arenas of authority?

What actions do the relevant social institutions demand?

Micro-and Macro-level Outcomes

How are individuals likely to behave?

How do these choices aggregate to affect outcomes?

Figure 2 Process of inquiry

they are relevant, one needs to recognize the multiple meanings of actions and how they fit within individuals' memberships in different arenas.

Even when arenas are overlapping and their requirements stand in opposition to each other, not all arenas are equally important. Whether or not decisions are driven by one arena or the other, or torn between them, depends on their strength. Institutions are likely stronger when there is solidarity among community members, the arena affects a larger extent of members' lives (e.g., is encompassing), and the community is able to monitor and sanction its members. The proximity of members to each other, and the networks among them, enhances such monitoring and enforcement. Arenas may also have greater or lesser sway over individuals, depending on individuals' means. Where individuals are wealthier, more educated, or more mobile, they are likely to be able to escape obligations put upon them.

Finally, the effects of these arenas depend on the specific roles, rules, and rewards within them. These include boundary rules (e.g., governing entry and exit to the community, as well as group boundary maintenance), rules of engagement (e.g., expectations with regard to interacting with insiders and outsiders), and leadership selection rules. The details are too nuanced to discuss in depth. However, as Section 5 illustrated, it is possible to consider the broad implications of categories of rules, much as scholars do with regard to regime types, electoral systems, and other state institutions.

7.2.2 Unanswered Questions

This perspective also raises a number of questions that require future research. Some questions are familiar, although they generally have been reserved for the state: how do the familiar dimensions of states – the strength or design of institutions – affect when and how individuals respond, to what effect? How does codification (i.e., moving from informal to formal, or parchment, rules) of non-state institutions affect behavior and development? How does the nature of leadership – the level of hierarchy, exclusivity, or turnover – affect outcomes? How do changes in technology, ideology, and material resources affect the power of alternative arenas over individuals, promote contestation over and changes in social institutions within them, or lead to the emergence of new arenas of authority altogether?

Other questions are new, the result of shifting the perspective from one in which the state is juxtaposed to less-fully theorized 'non-state' actors to one of multiple, potentially competing arenas. To what extent do changes in the social institutions of one arena lead to changes in other arenas as well? How do we understand 'bridge' actors – those whose role links various arenas of authority, such as the party candidates who are simultaneously local elites or sectarian group members described in Section 5? Bridge actors play important roles in multiple arenas and are constrained by social institutions within them, but how does exercising these roles affect their power in different arenas? Moreover, as elites within competing arenas of authority seek different responses from members they have in common, when do they compete, leading to potential escalation, and when do they concede, compromise, or even find mutually beneficial collaboration? Scholars have traditionally considered the relationship between the state and social arenas of authority, asking whether these are complements or substitutes (Migdal, 1988; Migdal et al., 1994). These questions about substitutability and complementarity can be asked regarding the multiple arenas outside the state as well.

A third set of questions centres on the aggregation of individuals' choices to political and development outcomes. Under what conditions does the threat of intervention from another arena alter the nature of power and dynamics in another? Examining Lagos, for instance, Shelby Grossman (2021) argues that the threat of state intervention improves accountability in informal trading associations. Under what conditions do such outcomes transfer to other arenas? Do outcomes change when arenas are nested (i.e., such that members of one arena are all equally members of the second one) or are cross-cutting (i.e., where some, but not all, members of the first arena are also members of the second)? When, and why, do overlapping arenas of authority enhance or inhibit coordination and collective action of individuals within a geographical locality? How does the belonging of individuals to different arenas, or the stratification and inequalities within single arenas, affect whether individuals can pull together to produce local public goods?

Finally, the framework raises new theoretical questions about the state. Students of politics tell a story of state-building that focuses on contestation between the state and social arenas, with the predominant state the best outcome. Yet, a closer view of social arenas suggests that the dominant state is often a fiction, sustained by mismeasure and international norms (importantly, authored by states). For those interested in the state, this opens questions over what factors provoke a re-ordering of the relations, a back and forth in the relative power of the state versus various social arenas over individuals' choices, and when they do so. The answers to such questions may help to illuminate changes not only in the states of the Global South, but in the West as well.

7.2.3 Methodological Challenges and Opportunities

This approach has methodological implications as well. It raises new measurement challenges. Given the value of social institutions and the subnational variation across them, it implies a move away from selective, single-realm judgements of quality of governance (e.g., fragile state indices). These, and even more extensive multi-sectoral measures, can permit us only a measure of governance and development. If governance takes place outside the state, to greater and lesser extents, then the study and practice of development requires metrics that take into account state and social arenas, tap into the relative importance and designs of these different arenas, and facilitate a mapping from arenas to outcomes.

Research must be well-grounded in case contexts. Scholars cannot assume that voting, service provision, or other behaviours have the same meaning across space, time, or individuals. Rather, they need to understand how individuals attach meaning to the acts at hand, and the extent to which these meanings, as well as the strength of relevant arenas of authority and the nature of their social institutions, vary. This does not negate the usefulness of experimental or large-N analyses. However, it does require such research to be based on a careful understanding of the context and suggests that value of interdisciplinary research built upon both qualitative and quantitative methods.

Some contexts may be particularly fruitful for such research. Cities bring these theoretical issues to the fore, particularly in the rapidly urbanizing Global South. Scholars have long recognized cities as spaces in which members of ethnic, religious, or other arenas of authority come together, often maintaining or reshaping their social institutions (Cohen et al., 1974), and more recently, viewed urban spaces as a site for contestation over '*who* has the legitimacy to govern a people and on the basis of *what* identity categories' as well (Davis and Libertun de Duren, 2011, p. 2). These sites thus raise important questions about how migration affects the strength or shape of arenas of authority, leading, for instance, to the transplantation of arenas of authority into urban spaces or the emergence of cross-cutting cleavages.

Boundary changes may offer similarly elucidating circumstances. Studies exploiting boundaries have often focused on how state boundaries, such as national borders or electoral constituencies, affect the salience of social arenas and individuals' behaviours (e.g., Chandra, 2007; Posner, 2005); however, exploring (changing) boundaries of social arenas may be equally enlightening. Much might also be learned by examining boundaries of social arenas, which might reconfigure given changes in boundary rules (e.g., rules of religious conversion, tribal association).

7.3 Towards Effective Development

The approach outlined here benefits scholars and practitioners alike. For scholars, it provides new insights into studies of both the state and social forces.

Studies that focus solely on the impact of political institutions on outcomes are likely to attribute far more import to the political institutions than is warranted. So too, efforts to understand the role of identity or to link identities and social conditions – such as economic inequalities or rural–urban divides – are incomplete unless they consider the relationship between such identities and overlapping arenas of authority.

This perspective also provides important insights for practitioners. It helps to explain why isomorphic mimicry, or the adoption of state organizational forms or policies that appear to be 'modern' or 'best practices', can result in zero improvement in state capability, or even decline (Pritchett et al., 2012). Quite simply, individuals implementing policies or engaging within these organizations may do so on the basis of arenas and social institutions outside the state, or indeed, attach very different meanings to engagement than the international practitioners and their local allies intended. The everyday approach to politics and development I present here also helps explain why advocates may face resistance in implementation. Where programmes and policies threaten the interests of elites in powerful arenas of authority outside the state, as they did in boundary making in Tunisia's decentralization process, for instance, they may not only face resistance but also spark unrest and even violence. Finally, the framework provides a basis for understanding why scholars find that informational interventions often to do not foster social accountability (Dunning et al., 2019). When individuals are subject to powerful incentives from arenas of authority outside the state, they may fail to hold officials and service providers accountable, even when they have full information.

The framework not only explains such potential outcomes but also provides a means for accumulating knowledge and improving programme design. Practitioners have increasingly recognized the importance of context, as it has become clear that programmes which worked splendidly in one area or country do poorly elsewhere. Indeed, even programmes that work well in one place at one time fail to do so in subsequent iterations. However, the response to date does not provide a strong foundation for learning from past experiences. For example, Matt Andrews, Lant Pritchett, and Michael Woolcock (2017) propose a problem-driven iterative adaptation (PDIA) method, in which practitioners identify multiple ideas, trying them out in an experimental process that allows for the emergence of hybrid solutions. The approach put forth here goes beyond the goal of PDIA's incremental and experimental approach. I anticipate that it is possible to develop a firmer understanding of politics and development such that lessons can be drawn and transferred to new places and times.

Advancing research and development programming requires revising insufficient and often state-centric theories, recognizing the ranges of authorities at play, and the nature of institutions associated with them. It starts by interrogating assumptions about how individuals understand the everyday choices before them and considering how the roles, rules, and rewards in multiple, competing arenas of authority influence their behaviour. If scholars and practitioners can identify systematic differences in the nature of arenas and social institutions that shape individuals' choices and, ultimately, development outcomes, then they can begin to ask the right questions, design better research, and develop appropriate programmes from the outset. The framework I have presented here, and the process of inquiry that follows from it, provide a basis for such efforts.

References

Acemoglu, D., Reed, T. and Robinson, J. A. (2014) 'Chiefs: Economic Development and Elite Control of Civil Society in Sierra Leone', *Journal of Political Economy*, 122(2), pp. 319–68. https://doi.org/10.1086/674988.

Acemoglu, D. and Robinson, J. A. (2012) *Why Nations Fail: The Origins of Power, Prosperity and Poverty*. 1st ed. New York: Crown.

Acker, J. (2012) 'Gendered Organizations and Intersectionality: Problems and Possibilities', *Equality, Diversity and Inclusion: An International Journal*, 31 (3), pp. 214–24. https://doi.org/10.1108/02610151211209072.

Agnew, J. (2005) 'Sovereignty Regimes: Territoriality and State Authority in Contemporary World Politics', *Annals of the Association of American Geographers*, 95(2), pp. 437–61.

Ahmad, J., Devarajan, S., Khemani, S. and Shah, S. (2005) *Decentralization and Service Delivery*. 3603, Policy Research Working Paper. Washington, DC: World Bank Group. https://openknowledge.worldbank.org/handle/10986/8933.

Al-Azzam, A. A. (2012) 'The Reality of Political Culture in Jordan after Twenty Years of Political Openness', *Journal of Social and Development Sciences*, 3 (10), pp. 350–9.

Albrecht, P. and Wiuff Moe, L. (2015) 'The Simultaneity of Authority in Hybrid Orders', *Peacebuilding*, 3(1), pp. 1–16. https://doi.org/10.1080/21647259.2014.928551.

Almond, G. A. and Verba, S. (1963) *The Civic Culture: Political Attitudes and Democracy in Five Nations*. Princeton, NJ: Princeton University Press. www.jstor.org/stable/j.ctt183pnr2 (accessed 31 July 2021).

Almond, G. A. and Verba, S. (1965) *The Civic Culture: Political Attitudes and Democracy in Five Nations, an Analytic Study*. Later printing ed. Boston, MA: Little, Brown.

Ambec, S. (2008) 'Voting over Informal Risk-Sharing Rules', *Journal of African Economies*, 17(4), pp. 635–59. https://doi.org/10.1093/jae/ejn001.

Andrews, M., Pritchett, L. and Woolcock, M. (2017) *Building State Capability: Evidence, Analysis, Action*. Oxford; New York: Oxford University Press.

Anthias, F. (2013) 'Intersectional What? Social Divisions, Intersectionality and Levels of Analysis', *Ethnicities*, 13(1), pp. 3–19. https://doi.org/10.1177/1468796812463547.

Arab Barometer (2019) *Country Report Jordan*. Arab Barometer Wave V. www.arabbarometer.org/wp-content/uploads/ABV_Jordan_Report_Public-Opinion_2019.pdf?ct=t%28What+Jordanians+Think_COPY_08%29&mc_cid=b997daec47&mc_eid=%5BUNIQID%5D.

Arends, H. (2020) 'The Dangers of Fiscal Decentralization and Public Service Delivery: A Review of Arguments', *Politische Vierteljahresschrift*, 61(3), pp. 599–622. https://doi.org/10.1007/s11615-020-00233-7.

Arias, E. Balan, P., Larreguy, H., Marshakl, J., and Querubin, P. (2019) 'Information Provision, Voter Coordination, and Electoral Accountability: Evidence from Mexican Social Networks', *American Political Science Review*, 113(2), pp. 475–98. https://doi.org/10.1017/S0003055419000091.

Arjona, A. (2016) *Rebelocracy: Social Order in the Colombian Civil War*. Ithaca, NY: Cornell University Press.

Arjona, A., Kasfir, N. and Mampilly, Z. (2015) *Rebel Governance in Civil War*. Cambridge: Cambridge University Press.

Aspinall, E. and Sukmajati, M. (eds.) (2016) *Electoral Dynamics in Indonesia: Money Politics, Patronage and Clientelism at the Grassroots*. Singapore: NUS Press.

Auerbach, A. M. (2019) *Demanding Development: The Politics of Public Goods Provision in India's Urban Slums*. 1st ed. Cambridge: Cambridge University Press. https://doi.org/10.1017/9781108649377.

Axelrod, R. M. (1984) *The Evolution of Cooperation*. New York: Basic Books.

Baldwin, K. (2016) *The Paradox of Traditional Chiefs in Democratic Africa*. Cambridge Studies in Comparative Politics. New York: Cambridge University Press.

Ball, R. (2001) 'Individualism, Collectivism, and Economic Development', *The Annals of the American Academy of Political and Social Science*, 573, pp. 57–84.

Bardhan, P. and Mookherjee, D. (2006) 'Decentralisation and Accountability in Infrastructure Delivery in Developing Countries', *The Economic Journal*, 116(508), pp. 101–27. https://doi.org/10.1111/j.1468-0297.2006.01049.x.

Baylouny, A. M. (2010) *Privatizing Welfare in the Middle East: Kin Mutual Aid Associations in Jordan and Lebanon*. Bloomington; Indianapolis: Indiana University Press.

Beetham, D. (1991) 'Max Weber and the Legitimacy of the Modern State', *Analyse & Kritik*, 13(1), pp. 34–45.

Bejarano, C., Brown, D. E., Allen Gershon, S. and Montoya, C. (2021) 'Shared Identities: Intersectionality, Linked Fate, and Perceptions of Political

Candidates', *Political Research Quarterly*, 74(4), pp. 970–85. https://doi.org/10.1177/1065912920951640.

Belaam, N. (2012) *The Case of Tunisian Elections Following the Arab Spring*. Congress 2012: Accelerating Excellence. ESOMAR. https://ana.esomar.org/documents/the-case-of-tunisian-elections-following-the-arab-spring (accessed 20 May 2020).

Bell, D. C. and Cox, M. L. (2015) 'Social Norms: Do We Love Norms Too Much?' *Journal of Family Theory & Review*, 7(1), pp. 28–46. https://doi.org/10.1111/jftr.12059.

Benford, R. D. and Snow, D. A. (2000) 'Framing Processes and Social Movements: An Overview and Assessment', *Annual Review of Sociology*, 26, pp. 611–39.

Benstead, L. J. (2016) 'Why Quotas Are Needed to Improve Women's Access to Services in Clientelistic Regimes', *Governance*, 29(2), pp. 185–205. https://doi.org/10.1111/gove.12162.

Berge, E., Kambewa, D., Munthali, A., and Wiig, H. (2014) 'Lineage and Land Reforms in Malawi: Do Matrilineal and Patrilineal Landholding Systems Represent a Problem for Land Reforms in Malawi?' *Land Use Policy*, 41, pp. 61–9. https://doi.org/10.1016/j.landusepol.2014.05.003.

Bjarnegård, E. (2013) *Gender, Informal Institutions and Political Recruitment: Explaining Male Dominance in Parliamentary Representation*. Basingstoke: Palgrave Macmillan.

Björkman, M. and Svensson, J. (2010) 'When Is Community-Based Monitoring Effective? Evidence from a Randomized Experiment in Primary Health in Uganda', *Journal of the European Economic Association*, 8(2–3), pp. 571–81. https://doi.org/10.1111/j.1542-4774.2010.tb00527.x.

Boix, C. (1997) 'Political Parties and the Supply Side of the Economy: The Provision of Physical and Human Capital in Advanced Economies. 1960–90*', *Midwest Political Science Association*, 41(3), pp. 814–45.

Boix, C. (1999) 'Setting the Rules of the Game: The Choice of Electoral Systems in Advanced Democracies', *American Political Science Review*, 93(3), pp. 609–24.

Booth, D. and Golooba-Mutebi, F. (2012) 'Developmental Patrimonialism? The Case of Rwanda', *African Affairs*, 111(444), pp. 379–403. https://doi.org/10.1093/afraf/ads026.

Bowler, S., Brockington, D. and Donovan, T. (2001) 'Election Systems and Voter Turnout: Experiments in the United States', *The Journal of Politics*, 63(3), pp. 902–15.

Bowles, S. (2016) *The Moral Economy: Why Good Incentives Are No Substitute for Good Citizens*. The Castle Lectures in Ethics, Politics, and Economics. New Haven; London: Yale University Press.

Bowles, S., Choi, J.-K. and Hopfensitz, A. (2003) 'The Co-evolution of Individual Behaviors and Social Institutions', *Journal of Theoretical Biology*, 223(2), pp. 135–47. https://doi.org/10.1016/S0022-5193(03)00060-2.

Bruce, J. W. and Migot-Adholla, S. E. (1994) *Searching for Land Security in Africa*. Washington, DC: World Bank. https://documents1.worldbank .org/curated/en/630121468742824113/pdf/280431Opaper.pdf (accessed 23 August 2022).

Brulé, R. and Gaikwad, N. (2021) 'Culture, Capital, and the Political Economy Gender Gap: Evidence from Meghalaya's Matrilineal Tribes', *The Journal of Politics*, 83(3), pp. 834–50. https://doi.org/10.1086/711176.

Bueno de Mesquita, B., Smith, A., Siverson, R. M., and Morrow, J. D. (2003) *The Logic of Political Survival* Boston: MIT Press, 2003.

Bush, S. S. and Gao, E. (2017) 'Small Tribes, Big Gains: The Strategic Uses of Gender Quotas in the Middle East', *Comparative Politics*, 49(2), pp. 149–67. https://doi.org/10.5129/001041517820201323.

Cammett, M. (2014) *Compassionate Communalism: Welfare and Sectarianism in Lebanon*. Ithaca, NY: Cornell University Press.

Cammett, M. and MacLean, L. M. (eds.) (2014) *The Politics of Non-State Social Welfare*. Ithaca, NY: Cornell University Press. www.degruyter.com/docu ment/doi/10.7591/9780801470349/html (accessed 14 July 2021).

Carey, J. and Hix, S. (2013) 'Between Science and Engineering: Reflections on the APSA Presidential Task Force on Political Science, Electoral Rules, and Democratic Governance: Consequences of Electoral Rules for Patterns of Redistribution and Regulation', *Perspectives on Politics*, 11(3), pp. 820–4. https://doi.org/10.1017/S1537592713002181.

Carey, J. Hix, S., Htun, M., Mozaffar, S., Powell, G. B., Reynolds, A. (2013) 'Between Science and Engineering: Reflections on the APSA Presidential Task Force on Political Science, Electoral Rules, and Democratic Governance: Political Scientists as Electoral System Engineers', *Perspectives on Politics*, 11(3), pp. 827–40. https://doi.org/10.1017/S1537592713002247.

Carey, J. M. and Shugart, M. S. (1995) 'Incentives to Cultivate a Personal Vote: A Rank Ordering of Electoral Formulas', *Electoral Studies*, 14(4), pp. 417–39. https://doi.org/10.1016/0261-3794(94)00035-2.

Chabal, P. and Daloz, J.-P. (2006) *Culture Troubles: Politics and the Interpretation of Meaning*. Chicago, IL: University of Chicago Press.

Chandra, K. (2006) 'What Is Ethnic Identity and Does It Matter?' *Annual Review of Political Science*, 9(1), pp. 397–424. https://doi.org/10.1146/annurev.polisci.9.062404.170715.

Chandra, K. (2007) *Why Ethnic Parties Succeed: Patronage and Ethnic Head Counts in India*. 1st paperback version. Cambridge Studies in Comparative Politics. Cambridge: Cambridge University Press.

Cho, S., Crenshaw, K. W. and McCall, L. (2013) 'Toward a Field of Intersectionality Studies: Theory, Applications, and Praxis', *Signs: Journal of Women in Culture and Society*, 38(4), pp. 785–810. https://doi.org/10.1086/669608.

Cingolani, L. (2018) 'The Role of State Capacity in Development Studies', *Journal of Development Perspectives*, 2(1–2), pp. 88–114. https://doi.org/10.5325/jdevepers.2.1-2.0088.

Clark, J. A. (2004) *Islam, Charity, and Activism: Middle-Class Networks and Social Welfare in Egypt, Jordan, and Yemen*. Indiana Series in Middle East Studies. Bloomington: Indiana University Press.

Cleaver, F., Franks, T., Maganga, F. and Hall, K. (2013) 'Institutions, Security, and Pastoralism: Exploring the Limits of Hybridity', *African Studies Review*, 56(3), pp. 165–89.

Cohen, A. and Association of Social Anthropologists of the Commonwealth (eds.) (1974) *Urban Ethnicity*. A. S. A. Monographs 12. London; New York: Tavistock.

Cohen, C. J. (1999) *Boundaries of Blackness: AIDS and the Breakdown of Black Politics*. Chicago, IL: University of Chicago Press. https://archive.org/details/boundariesofblac00cohe (accessed 15 December 2021).

Corstange, D. (2016) *The Price of a Vote in the Middle East*. Cambridge: Cambridge University Press.

Cox, G. W. (1997) *Making Votes Count: Strategic Coordination in the World's Electoral Systems*. 1st ed. Cambridge: Cambridge University Press. https://doi.org/10.1017/CBO9781139174954.

Cox, G. W. (2015) 'Electoral Rules, Mobilization, and Turnout', *Annual Review of Political Science*, 18(1), pp. 49–68. https://doi.org/10.1146/annurev-polisci-060414-035915.

Crary, D. (2019) 'Women Strive for Larger Roles in Male-Dominated Religions', *Religion News Service*, 15 January. https://religionnews.com/2019/01/15/women-strive-for-larger-roles-in-male-dominated-religions/ (accessed 12 July 2021).

Crenshaw, K. (1990) 'Mapping the Margins: Intersectionality, Identity Politics, and Violence against Women of Color', *Stanford Law Review*, 43(6), pp. 1241–300.

Cruz, C. (2019) 'Social Networks and the Targeting of Vote Buying', *Comparative Political Studies*, 52(3), pp. 382–411. https://doi.org/10.1177/0010414018784062.

Cruz, C., Labonne, J. and Querubín, P. (2020) 'Social Network Structures and the Politics of Public Goods Provision: Evidence from the Philippines', *American Political Science Review*, 114(2), pp. 486–501. https://doi.org/10.1017/S0003055419000789.

Davis, D. E. and Libertun de Duren, N. (eds.) (2011) *Cities & Sovereignty: Identity Politics in Urban Spaces*. Bloomington: Indiana University Press.

Dawson, M. C. (1995) *Behind the Mule: Race and Class in African-American Politics*. 1st paperback print. Princeton, NJ: Princeton University Press.

Deutsch, K. W. (1961) 'Social Mobilization and Political Development', *American Political Science Review*, 55(3), pp. 493–514.

Díaz-Cayeros, A., Magaloni, B. and Ruiz-Euler, A. (2014) 'Traditional Governance, Citizen Engagement, and Local Public Goods: Evidence from Mexico', *World Development*, 53, pp. 80–93. https://doi.org/10.1016/j.worlddev.2013.01.008.

Dionne, K. Y. (2018) *Doomed Interventions: The Failure of Global Responses to AIDS in Africa*. Cambridge: Cambridge University Press.

Doherty, M. (2012) *Building a New Libya: Citizen Views on Libya's Electoral and Political Processes*. National Democratic Institute. www.ndi.org/sites/default/files/Libya-Focus-Group-May2012.pdf (accessed 19 May 2020).

Doucouliagos, H. and Ulubaşoğlu, M. A. (2008) 'Democracy and Economic Growth: A Meta-Analysis', *American Journal of Political Science*, 52(1), pp. 61–83.

Dulani, B., Lust, E. and Swila, H. (2016) *Binding Constraints in Service Delivery in Malawi*. World Bank Report (Unpublished). Washington, DC: World Bank Group.

Dulani, B., Harris, A.S., Horowitz, J., and Kayuni, H. (2021) 'Electoral Preferences Among Multiethnic Voters in Africa', *Comparative Political Studies*, 54(2), pp. 280–311. https://doi.org/10.1177/0010414020926196.

Dunning, T., Grossman, G., Humphreys, M., Hyde, S. D., McIntosh, C. and Nellis, G. (eds.) (2019) *Information, Accountability, and Cumulative Learning: Lessons from Metaketa I*. 1st ed. Cambridge: Cambridge University Press. https://doi.org/10.1017/9781108381390.

Ekeh, P. P. (1975) 'Colonialism and the Two Publics in Africa: A Theoretical Statement', *Comparative Studies in Society and History*, 17(1), pp. 91–112. https://doi.org/10.1017/S0010417500007659.

Ellickson, R. C. (1994) *Order without Law: How Neighbors Settle Disputes*. Cambridge, MA: Harvard University Press.

Englund, H. (ed.) (2002) *A Democracy of Chameleons: Politics and Culture in the New Malawi*. Uppsala: Nordiska Afrikainstitutet; Christian Literature Association in Malawi.

Esaiasson, P. and Sohlberg, J. (2020) *Caulking the Social Fabric: How National and Local Identities Promotes Pro-Social Attitudes in European Diverse and Disadvantaged Neighborhoods*. 29, The Program on Governance and Local Development Working Paper. Gothenburg: University of Gothenburg. https://gld.gu.se/media/1693/gld-working-paper-29-final.pdf

Fearon, J. D. and Laitin, D. D. (1996) 'Explaining Inter-Ethnic Cooperation', *American Political Science Review*, 90(4), pp. 715–35.

Ferrali, R. Grossman, G., Platas, M.R. and Rodden, J. (2019) 'It Takes a Village: Peer Effects and Externalities in Technology Adoption', *American Journal of Political Science*, 64, pp. 536–53. https://doi.org/10.1111/ajps.12471.

Ferree, K. E., Honig, L., Lust, E., and Phillips, M. (2022) 'Land and Legibility: When Do Citizens Expect Secure Property Rights in Weak States?' *American Political Science Review*, [Online First]. https://doi.org/10.1017/S0003055422000417.

Ferree, K. E., Powell, G. B. and Scheiner, E. (2013) 'Between Science and Engineering: Reflections on the APSA Presidential Task Force on Political Science, Electoral Rules, and Democratic Governance: How Context Shapes the Effects of Electoral Rules', *Perspectives on Politics*, 11(3), pp. 810–14. https://doi.org/10.1017/S153759271300220X.

Ferree, K. E., Powell, G. B. and Scheiner, E. (2014) 'Context, Electoral Rules, and Party Systems', *Annual Review of Political Science*, 17(1), pp. 421–39. https://doi.org/10.1146/annurev-polisci-102512-195419.

Finan, F. and Schechter, L. (2012) 'Vote-Buying and Reciprocity', *Econometrica*, 80(2), pp. 863–81.

Forsyth, M., Kent, L., Dinnen, S., Wallis, J., and Bose, S. (2017) 'Hybridity in Peacebuilding and Development: A Critical Approach'. *Third World Thematics: A TWQ Journal*, 2(4), pp. 407–21.

Fukuyama, F. (2004) 'The Imperative of State-Building', *Journal of Democracy*, 15(2), pp. 17–31. https://doi.org/10.1353/jod.2004.0026.

Gadjanova, E. (2017) 'Ethnic Wedge Issues in Electoral Campaigns in Africa's Presidential Regimes', *African Affairs*, 116(464), pp. 484–507. https://doi.org/10.1093/afraf/adx004.

Galvan, D. (1997) 'The Market Meets Sacred Fire: Land Pawning as Institutional Syncretism in Inter-War Senegal', *African Economic History*, 25, pp. 9–41. https://doi.org/10.2307/3601877.

Gao, E. (2016) 'Tribal Mobilization, Fragmented Groups, and Public Goods Provision in Jordan', *Comparative Political Studies*, 49(10), pp. 1372–403. https://doi.org/10.1177/0010414015621075.

Geddes, B., Wright, J. and Frantz, E. (2018) *How Dictatorships Work: Power, Personalization, and Collapse.* 1st ed. Cambridge: Cambridge University Press. https://doi.org/10.1017/9781316336182.

Gerring, J. Bond, P., Barndt, W. T., and Moreno, C. (2005) 'Democracy and Economic Growth: A Historical Perspective', *World Politics*, 57(3), pp. 323–64.

Gerschenkron, A. (1952) 'The Historical Approach to Economic Growth: Economic Backwardness in Historical Perspective', in Hoselitz, B. F. (ed.) *The Progress of Underdeveloped Areas.* Chicago, IL: University of Chicago Press.

Ghani, A. and Lockhart, C. (2009) *Fixing Failed States: A Framework for Rebuilding a Fractured World.* New York: Oxford University Press

Gluckman, M. (1973) *The Judicial Process Among the Barotse of Northern Rhodesia.* 2nd ed., reprinted with minor amendments. Manchester: Manchester University Press.

Gordon, S. C., Landa, D. and Bihan, P. L. (2015) *Crosscutting Cleavages and Political Conflict.* 15–30, Working Paper. Toulouse, France: Institute for Advanced Study in Toulouse. https://www.iast.fr/sites/default/files/IAST/IAST_V1/wp/wp_iast_1530.pdf (accessed 23 August 2022).

Granovetter, M. S. (1983) 'The Strength of Weak Ties: A Network Theory Revisited', *Sociological Theory*, 1, pp. 201–33. https://doi.org/10.2307/202051.

Granovetter, M. S. (1973) 'The Strength of Weak Ties', *American Journal of Sociology*, 78(6), pp. 1360–80.

Grossman, G. and Lewis, J. I. (2014) 'Administrative Unit Proliferation', *American Political Science Review*, 108(1), pp. 196–217. https://doi.org/10.1017/S0003055413000567.

Grossman, S. (2021) *The Politics of Order in Informal Markets: How the State Shapes Private Governance.* 1st ed. Cambridge: Cambridge University Press. https://doi.org/10.1017/9781108984980.

Gutmann, J. and Voigt, S. (2020) 'Traditional Law in Times of the Nation State: Why Is It so Prevalent?' *Journal of Institutional Economics*, 16(4), pp. 445–61. https://doi.org/10.1017/S1744137420000119.

Habyarimana, J. Humphreys, M., Posner, D., and Weinstein, J. (2007) 'Why Does Ethnic Diversity Undermine Public Goods Provision?' *American*

Political Science Review, 101(4), pp. 709–25. https://doi.org/10.1017/S0003055407070499.

Hale, H. E. (2004) 'Explaining Ethnicity', *Comparative Political Studies*, 37 (4), pp. 458–85. https://doi.org/10.1177/0010414003262906.

Hanandah, A. (2010) 'Al-asha'ir al-urdunniya alati methalat fi majalis al-nuab fi 63 'aaman' ('The Jordanian Tribes That are Represented in National Assemblies over 63 Years'), *Al-Madina*, 19 December. http://almadenah news.com/newss/news.php?c=532&id=64992 (accessed 19 December 2010).

Harper, E. (2011) *Customary Justice: From Program Design to Impact Evaluation*. Rome: International Development Law Organization.

Harris, A. S. (2022) *Everyday Identity and Electoral Politics: Race, Ethnicity, and the Bloc Vote in South Africa and Beyond*. Oxford: Oxford University Press.

Harris, A., Honig, L. (2022) 'Mutual Dependence and Expectations of Cooperation'. *The Journal of Politics*. https://doi.org/10.1086/720646.

Harsanyi, J. C. (1969) 'Rational-Choice Models of Political Behavior vs. Functionalist and Conformist Theories', *World Politics*, 21(4), pp. 513–38. https://doi.org/10.2307/2009665.

Helmke, G. and Levitsky, S. (2004) 'Informal Institutions and Comparative Politics: A Research Agenda', *Perspectives on Politics*, 2(4), pp. 725–40. https://doi.org/10.1017/S1537592704040472.

Helmke, G. and Levitsky, S. (eds.) (2006) *Informal Institutions and Democracy: Lessons from Latin America*. Baltimore, MD: Johns Hopkins University Press.

Henrich, J., Boyd, R., Bowles, S. S., Camerer, C., Fehr, E., Gintis, H. and McElreath, R. (2001) 'In Search of Homo Economicus: Behavioral Experiments in 15 Small-Scale Societies', *American Economic Review*, 91 (2), pp. 73–8. https://doi.org/10.1257/aer.91.2.73.

Hicken, A. and Nathan, N. L. (2020) 'Clientelism's Red Herrings: Dead Ends and New Directions in the Study of Nonprogrammatic Politics', *Annual Review of Political Science*, 23(1), pp. 277–94. https://doi.org/10.1146/annurev-polisci-050718-032657.

Hofstede, G. (1982) *Culture's Consequences: International Differences in Work-Related Values*. Newbury Park: Sage.

Htun, M. and Powell, G. B. (2013) 'Between Science and Engineering: Reflections on the APSA Presidential Task Force on Political Science, Electoral Rules, and Democratic Governance: Introduction', *Perspectives on Politics*, 11(3), pp. 808–10. https://doi.org/10.1017/S1537592713002065.

Hu, H.-H., Lin, J. and Cui, W. (2015) 'Cultural Differences and Collective Action: A Social Network Perspective', *Complexity*, 20(4), pp. 68–77. https://doi.org/10.1002/cplx.21515.

Huntington, S. P. (1968) *Political Order in Changing Societies*. New Haven, CT: Yale University Press

Inglehart, R. and Welzel, C. (2005) *Modernization, Cultural Change, and Democracy: The Human Development Sequence*. Cambridge: Cambridge University Press.

Inter-Parliamentary Union (1997) *Elections Held in 1997*. Inter-Parliamentary Union. http://archive.ipu.org/parline-e/reports/arc/2163_97.htm (accessed 30 July 2021).

Jackman, R. W. (1987) 'Political Institutions and Voter Turnout in the Industrial Democracies', *American Political Science Review*, 81(2), pp. 405–23. https://doi.org/10.2307/1961959.

Jackson, R. H. and Rosberg, C. G. (1984) 'Popular Legitimacy in African Multi-Ethnic States', *The Journal of Modern African Studies*, 22(2), pp. 177–98. https://doi.org/10.1017/S0022278X00056019.

Jaraba, M. (2020) '*Khul'* in Action: How Do Local Muslim Communities in Germany Dissolve an Islamic Religious-Only Marriage?' *Journal of Muslim Minority Affairs*, 40(1), pp. 26–47. https://doi.org/10.1080/13602004 .2020.1737414.

Joffé, G. (2012) *Elections in Libya*. 48, Brief. European Institute of the Mediterranean. www.iemed.org/wp-content/uploads/2020/12/EuroMeSCo-Policy-Brief-48-Elections-in-Libya.pdf (accessed 31 July 2021).

Jones-Casey, K. and Knox, A. (2011) *Ghana's Land Administration at a Crossroads*. Focus on Land in Africa Brief. Land Portal.

Jöst, P. (2021) 'Where Do the Less Affluent Vote? The Effect of Neighbourhood Social Context on Individual Voting Intentions in England', *Political Studies*. August 2021. https://doi.org/10.1177/00323217211027480.

Jöst, P. and Lust, E. (2022) *Leadership, Community Ties, and Participation of the Poor: Evidence from Kenya, Malawi, and Zambia*. 55, The Program on Governance and Local Development Working Paper. Gothenburg: University of Gothenburg. https://papers.ssrn.com/sol3/papers.cfm?abstract_id= 4046628 (accessed 23 August 2022).

Kam, C., Bertelli, A. M. and Held, A. (2020) 'The Electoral System, the Party System and Accountability in Parliamentary Government', *American Political Science Review*, 114(3), pp. 744–60. https://doi.org/10.1017/S000 3055420000143.

Kamwendo, G. H. (2002) 'Ethnic Revival and Language Associations in the New Malawi: The Case of Chitumbuka', in Englund, H. (ed.) *A Democracy of Chameleons: Politics and Culture in the New Malawi*. Uppsala: Nordic Africa Institute, pp. 140–50.

Kao, K. (2015) *Electoral Institutions, Ethnicity, and Clientelism: Authoritarianism in Jordan*. PhD Thesis. University of California. https://escholarship.org/content/qt829340k4/qt829340k4_noSplash_25da3a01c097b44d692e3a748102a79e.pdf?t=nyq6mk (accessed 6 June 2021).

Kao, K., Lust, E., Dulani, B., Ferree, K. E., Harris, A. S. and Metheney, E. A. (2021) 'The ABCs of Covid-19 Prevention in Malawi: Authority, Benefits, and Costs of Compliance', *World Development*, 137, 105167. https://doi.org/10.1016/j.worlddev.2020.105167.

Kelman, H. and Hamilton, L. (1989) *Crimes of Obedience: Toward a Social Psychology of Authority and Responsibility*. New Haven, CT: Yale University Press.

Kelsall, T. (2008) 'Going with the Grain in African Development?' *Development Policy Review*, 26(6), pp.627–55. https://doi.org/10.1111/j.1467-7679.2008.00427.x.

Kelsall, T. (2012) 'Neo-Patrimonialism, Rent-Seeking and Development: Going with the Grain?' *New Political Economy*, 17(5), pp. 677–82. https://doi.org/10.1080/13563467.2012.732275.

Khan Mohmand, S. and Mihajlović, S. M. (2016) *Integrating Informal Institutions in Local Governance: Does It Matter?* Brighton UK, University of Sussex. 473, Working Paper. Institute of Development Studies. https://opendocs.ids.ac.uk/opendocs/handle/20.500.12413/12130 (accessed 27 January 2020).

Kherigi, I. (2021a) *Municipal Boundaries and the Politics of Space in Tunisia*. 38, The Program on Governance and Local Development Working Paper. Gothenburg: University of Gothenburg.

Kherigi, I. (2021b) *Who Decides in Today's Tunisia? Analyzing the Construction of Decentralization Reforms in Post-revolution Tunisia*. Paris: Institut d'études politiques de Paris.

Knutsen, C. H. and Nygård, H. M. (2015) 'Institutional Characteristics and Regime Survival: Why Are Semi-Democracies Less Durable Than Autocracies and Democracies?' *American Journal of Political Science*, 59 (3), pp. 656–70. https://doi.org/10.1111/ajps.12168.

Krasner, S. D. (2011) 'International Support for State-Building', *PRISM*, 2(3), pp. 65–74.

Krook, M. L. (2018) 'Electoral Systems and Women's Representation', in Herron, E. S., Pekkanen, R. J. and Shugart, M. S. (eds.) *The Oxford Handbook of Electoral Systems*. Oxford, England: Oxford University Press, pp. 174–92. https://doi.org/10.1093/oxfordhb/9780190258658.013.27.

Krook, M. L. and Moser, R. G. (2013) 'Between Science and Engineering: Reflections on the APSA Presidential Task Force on Political Science, Electoral Rules, and Democratic Governance: Electoral Rules and Political Inclusion', *Perspectives on Politics*, 11(3), pp. 814–18. https://doi.org/10.1017/S1537592713002211.

Kruks-Wisner, G. (2018) *Claiming the State: Active Citizenship and Social Welfare in Rural India*. Cambridge: Cambridge University Press. https://doi.org/10.1017/9781108185899.

Kutsoati, E. and Morck, R. (2016) *Family Ties, Inheritance Rights, and Successful Poverty Alleviation: Evidence from Ghana*. Chicago, IL: University of Chicago Press. www.degruyter.com/document/doi/10.7208/9780226316192-009/html (accessed 10 May 2021).

Lawler, E. J. (1992) 'Affective Attachments to Nested Groups: A Choice-Process Theory', *American Sociological Review*, 57(3), pp. 327–39. https://doi.org/10.2307/2096239.

Lawler, E. J., Thye, S. R. and Yoon, J. (2016) 'The Problem of Social Order in Nested Group Structures', in Abrutyn, S. (ed.) *Handbook of Contemporary Sociological Theory*. Handbooks of Sociology and Social Research. Cham: Springer International, pp. 149–66. https://doi.org/10.1007/978-3-319-32250-6_8.

Lawson, C. and Greene, K. F. (2014) 'Making Clientelism Work: How Norms of Reciprocity Increase Voter Compliance', *Comparative Politics*, 47(1), pp. 61–77.

Ledeneva, A. (2008) '*Blat* and *Guanxi*: Informal Practices in Russia and China', *Comparative Studies in Society and History*, 50(1), pp. 118–44. https://doi.org/10.1017/S0010417508000078.

Legros, S. and Cislaghi, B. (2020) 'Mapping the Social-Norms Literature: An Overview of Reviews', *Perspectives on Psychological Science*, 15(1), pp. 62–80. https://doi.org/10.1177/1745691619866455.

Lerner, D. (1958) *The Passing of Traditional Society: Modernizing the Middle East*. Glencoe, Ill.: Free Press.

Levy, B. (2014) *Working with the Grain: Integrating Governance and Growth in Development Strategies*. New York: Oxford University Press.

Lieberman, E. S. (2009) *Boundaries of Contagion: How Ethnic Politics Have Shaped Government Responses to AIDS*. Princeton, NJ: Princeton University Press.

Lijphart, A. (1977) *Democracy in Plural Societies: A Comparative Exploration*. New Haven, CT: Yale University Press.

Lipset, S. M. (1959) 'Some Social Requisites of Democracy: Economic Development and Political Legitimacy', *American Political Science Review*, 53(1), pp. 69–105. https://doi.org/10.2307/1951731.

Lipset, S. M. (1960) *Political Man: The Social Bases of Politics*. Garden City, NY: Doubleday.

Lipset, S. M. and Rokkan, S. (1967) *Party Systems and Voter Alignments: Cross-National Perspectives*. Toronto: The Free Press.

Liu, S. S., Morris, M. W., Talhelm, T., Yang Q. (2019) 'Ingroup Vigilance in Collectivistic Cultures', *Proceedings of the National Academy of Sciences*, 116(29), pp. 14538–46. https://doi.org/10.1073/pnas.18175 88116.

Logan, C. (2013) 'The Roots of Resilience: Exploring Popular Support for African Traditional Authorities', *African Affairs*, 112(448), pp. 353–76. https://doi.org/10.1093/afraf/adt025.

Lust, E., Hourani, S. and El-Moumani, M. (2011) 'Jordan Votes: Election or Selection?' *Journal of Democracy*, 22(2), pp. 119–29.

Lust, E., Kao, K., Landry, P. et al. (2019) *The Local Governance Performance Index (LGPI): Kenya, Malawi, Zambia*. The Program on Governance and Local Development, University of Gothenburg. https://gld.gu.se.

Lust-Okar, E. (2006) 'Elections under Authoritarianism: Preliminary Lessons from Jordan', *Democratization*, 13(3), pp. 456–71. https://doi.org/10.1080/13510340600579359.

Lust-Okar, E. (2009) 'Reinforcing Informal Institutions through Authoritarian Elections: Insights from Jordan', *Middle East Law and Governance*, 1(1), pp. 3–37. https://doi.org/10.1163/187633708X339444.

Mac Ginty, R., and Richmond, O. (2016) 'The Fallacy of Constructing Hybrid Political Orders: A Reappraisal of the Hybrid Turn in Peacebuilding'. *International Peacekeeping*, 23(2), 219–39.

MacLean, L. M. (2010) *Informal Institutions and Citizenship in Rural Africa: Risk and Reciprocity in Ghana and Côte d'Ivoire*. Cambridge Studies in Comparative Politics. Cambridge: Cambridge University Press. https://doi.org/10.1017/CBO9780511730368.

Magaloni, B. (2008) 'Credible Power-Sharing and the Longevity of Authoritarian Rule', *Comparative Political Studies*, 41(4–5), pp. 715–41. https://doi.org/10.1177/0010414007313124.

Magaloni, B., Franco-Vivanco, E. and Melo, V. (2020) 'Killing in the Slums: Social Order, Criminal Governance, and Police Violence in Rio de Janeiro', *American Political Science Review*, 114(2), pp. 552–72. https://doi.org/10.1017/S0003055419000856.

Mainwaring, S. and Scully, T. (1995) *Building Democratic Institutions: Party Systems in Latin America*. Stanford: Stanford University Press.

March, J. G. and Olsen, J. P. (1984) 'The New Institutionalism: Organizational Factors in Political Life', *American Political Science Review*, 78(3), pp. 734–49. https://doi.org/10.2307/1961840.

Mares, I. and Young, L. (2016) 'Buying, Expropriating, and Stealing Votes', *Annual Review of Political Science*, 19(1), pp. 267–88. https://doi.org/10.1146/annurev-polisci-060514-120923.

Markus, H. R. and Kitayama, S. (1991) 'Culture and the Self: Implications for Cognition, Emotion, and Motivation', *Psychological Review*, 98(2), pp. 224–53. https://doi.org/10.1037/0033-295X.98.2.224.

Mazzucato, V. and Kabki, M. (2009) 'Small Is Beautiful: The Micro-Politics of Transnational Relationships between Ghanaian Hometown Associations and Communities Back Home', *Global Networks*, 9(2), pp. 227–51. https://doi.org/10.1111/j.1471-0374.2009.00252.x.

McCauley, J. F. and Posner, D. N. (2019) 'The Political Sources of Religious Identification: Evidence from the Burkina Faso–Côte d'Ivoire Border', *British Journal of Political Science*, 49(2), pp. 421–41. https://doi.org/10.1017/S0007123416000594.

McGinnis, M. D. and Ostrom, E. (2011) 'Reflections on Vincent Ostrom, Public Administration, and Polycentricity', *Public Administration Review*, 72(1), pp. 15–25. https://doi.org/10.1111/j.1540-6210.2011.02488.x.

McLaughlin, E. S. (2007) 'Beyond the Racial Census: The Political Salience of Ethnolinguistic Cleavages in South Africa', *Comparative Political Studies*, 40(4), pp. 435–56. https://doi.org/10.1177/0010414006294420.

Miettunen, P. and Shunnaq, M. (2020) *Tribal Networks and Informal Adaptive Mechanisms of Syrian Refugees: The Case of the Bani Khalid Tribe in Jordan, Syria and Lebanon*. Beirut: Issam Fares Institute for Public Policy and International Affairs (IFI) at the American University of Beirut (AUB).

Migdal, J. S. (1988) *Strong Societies and Weak States: State-Society Relations and State Capabilities in the Third World*. Princeton, NJ: Princeton University Press.

Migdal, J. S., Kohli, A. and Shue, V. (eds.) (1994) *State Power and Social Forces: Domination and Transformation in the Third World*. Cambridge Studies in Comparative Politics. Cambridge; New York: Cambridge University Press.

Miguel, E. and Gugerty, M. K. (2005) 'Ethnic Diversity, Social Sanctions, and Public Goods in Kenya', *Journal of Public Economics*, 89(11), pp. 2325–68. https://doi.org/10.1016/j.jpubeco.2004.09.004.

Miller, S. (2019) 'Social Institutions', *The Standford Encyclopedia of Philosophy*. https://plato.stanford.edu/archives/sum2019/entries/social-institutions/ (accessed 28 April 2020).

Mitchell, T. (1991) 'The Limits of the State: Beyond Statist Approaches and Their Critics', *American Political Science Review*, 85(1), pp. 77–96. https://doi.org/10.2307/1962879 (accessed 23 August 2022).

Murtazashvili, J. B. (2016) *Informal Order and the State in Afghanistan*. Cambridge: Cambridge University Press.

National Democratic Institute (2010) *Final International Election Observation*. National Democratic Institute.

Nordlinger, E. A. (1981) *On the Autonomy of the Democratic State*. Cambridge, MA: Harvard University Press.

Norris, P. (1997) 'Choosing Electoral Systems: Proportional, Majoritarian and Mixed Systems', *International Political Science Review*, 18(3), pp. 297–312. https://doi.org/10.1177/019251297018003005.

North, D. C. (1990) *Institutions, Institutional Change, and Economic Performance*. The Political Economy of Institutions and Decisions. Cambridge; New York: Cambridge University Press.

Obeng-Odoom, F. (2015) 'Understanding Land Grabs in Africa: Insights from Marxist and Georgist Political Economics', *The Review of Black Political Economy*, 42(4), pp. 337–54. https://doi.org/10.1007/s12114-015-9209-2.

Olson, M. (1965) *The Logic of Collective Action: Public Goods and the Theory of Groups*. 21st print. Harvard Economic Studies 124. Cambridge, MA: Harvard University Press.

Olson, M. (1993) 'Dictatorship, Democracy, and Development', *American Political Science Review*, 87(3), pp. 567–76.

Ostrom, E. (1990) *Governing the Commons: The Evolution of Institutions for Collective Action*. The Political Economy of Institutions and Decisions. Cambridge: Cambridge University Press.

Ostrom, E. (2005) *Understanding Institutional Diversity*. Princeton, NJ: Princeton University Press.

Ostrom, E. (2010) 'Beyond Markets and States: Polycentric Governance of Complex Economic Systems', *American Economic Review*, 100(3), pp. 641–72. https://doi.org/10.1257/aer.100.3.641.

Ostrom, E. and Janssen, M. A. (2004) 'Multi-Level Governance and Resilience of Social-Ecological Systems', in Spoor, M. (ed.) *Globalisation, Poverty and Conflict: A Critical 'Development' Reader*. Dordrecht: Springer, pp. 239–59. https://doi.org/10.1007/1-4020-2858-X_13.

Ostrom, V., Tiebout, C. M. and Warren, R. (1961) 'The Organization of Government in Metropolitan Areas: A Theoretical Inquiry', *American Political Science Review*, 55(4), pp. 831–42. https://doi.org/10.2307/1952530 (accessed 23 August 2022).

Paller, J. W. (2019) *Democracy in Ghana: Everyday Politics in Urban Africa.* 1st ed. Cambridge: Cambridge University Press. https://doi.org/10.1017/9781108578721.

Pankani, W. (2014) *System Overload: A Reversed Collective Action Dilemma in Botswana and Ghana.* PhD Dissertation. University of Florida.

Parsons, T. E. (1951) *Toward a General Theory of Action.* Cambridge, MA: Harvard University Press. https://doi.org/10.4159/harvard.9780674863507.

Patel, D. S. (2015) *The More Things Change, the More They Stay the Same: Jordanian Islamist Responses in Spring and Fall.* Rethinking Political Islam Series. Washington, DC: Brookings Institute.

Piff, P. K. and Robinson, A. R. (2017) 'Social Class and Prosocial Behavior: Current Evidence, Caveats, and Questions', *Current Opinion in Psychology*, 18, pp. 6–10. https://doi.org/10.1016/j.copsyc.2017.06.003.

Piff, P. K. Kraus, M. W., Côté, S., Cheng, B. H., and Keltner, D. (2010) 'Having Less, Giving More: The Influence of Social Class on Prosocial Behavior', *Journal of Personality and Social Psychology*, 99(5), pp. 771–84. https://doi.org/10.1037/a0020092.

Piff, P. K., Stancato, D. M., Côté, S., Mendoza-Denton, R., and Keltner, D. (2012) 'Higher Social Class Predicts Increased Unethical Behavior', *Proceedings of the National Academy of Sciences*, 109(11), pp. 4086–91. https://doi.org/10.1073/pnas.1118373109.

Posner, D. N. (2005) *Institutions and Ethnic Politics in Africa.* Political Economy of Institutions and Decisions. Cambridge; New York: Cambridge University Press.

Post, A. E., Bronsoler, V. and Salman, L. (2017) 'Hybrid Regimes for Local Public Goods Provision: A Framework for Analysis', *Perspectives on Politics*, 15(4), pp. 952–66. https://doi.org/10.1017/S1537592717002109.

Povoledo, E. (2021) 'Pope Formalizes Women's Roles, but Priesthood Stays Out of Reach', *The New York Times*, 11 January. www.nytimes.com/2021/01/11/world/europe/pope-women.html (accessed 12 July 2021).

Presthus, R. V. (1960) 'The Sociology of Economic Development', *International Journal of Comparative Sociology*, 1(2), pp. 195–201.

Pritchett, L., Woolcock, M. and Andrews, M. (2012) *Looking Like a State: Techniques of Persistent Failure in State Capability for Implementation.* 239, CID Working Paper. Cambridge, MA: Harvard University.

Przeworski, A. (ed.) (2000) *Democracy and Development: Political Institutions and Well-Being in the World, 1950–1990.* Cambridge Studies in the Theory of Democracy. Cambridge: Cambridge University Press.

Putnam, R. D. (1993) 'The Prosperous Community: Social Capital and Public Life', *The American Prospect*, 13, pp. 35–42.

Putnam, R. D. (2000) *Bowling Alone: The Collapse and Revival of American Community*. New York: Simon and Schuster.

Putnam, R. D., Leonardi, R. and Nanetti, R. (1994) *Making Democracy Work: Civic Traditions in Modern Italy*. 5th print, 1st Princeton paperback print. Princeton, NJ: Princeton University Press.

Rae, D. W. and Taylor, M. (1970) *The Analysis of Political Cleavages*. New Haven, CT: Yale University Press.

Raffler, P., Posner, D. N. and Parkerson, D. (2020) *Can Citizen Pressure Be Induced to Improve Public Service Provision?* Innovations for Poverty Action Working Paper. www.poverty-action.org/publication/can-citizen-pressure-be-induced-improve-public-service-provision (accessed August 23, 2022).

Ravanilla, N., Haim, D. and Hicken, A. (2021) 'Brokers, Social Networks, Reciprocity, and Clientelism', *American Journal of Political Science*. https://doi.org/10.1111/ajps.12604.

Repetto, T. A. (1974) *Residential Crime*. Cambridge: Ballinger.

Robinson, A. L. and Gottlieb, J. (2019) 'How to Close the Gender Gap in Political Participation: Lessons from Matrilineal Societies in Africa', *British Journal of Political Science*, 51(1), pp. 68–92. https://doi.org/10.1017/S0007123418000650.

Rustow, D. A. (1970) 'Transitions to Democracy: Toward a Dynamic Model', *Comparative Politics*, 2(3), pp. 337–63. https://doi.org/10.2307/421307.

Sampson, R. J., Morenoff, J. D. and Felton, E. (1999) 'Beyond Social Capital: Spatial Dynamics of Collective Efficacy for Children', *American Sociological Review*, 64(5), pp. 633–60. https://doi.org/10.2307/2657367.

Sandefur, J. and Siddiqi, B. (2013) 'Delivering Justice to the Poor: Theory and Experimental Evidence from Liberia', at *World Bank Workshop on African Political Economy*, Washington, DC, May.

Sanz, C. (2017) 'The Effect of Electoral Systems on Voter Turnout: Evidence from a Natural Experiment', *Political Science Research and Methods*, 5(4), pp. 689–710. https://doi.org/10.1017/psrm.2015.54.

Schaffer, F. C. (1998) *Democracy in Translation: Understanding Politics in an Unfamiliar Culture*. 1st ed. Ithaca, NY: Cornell University Press.

Schaffer, F. C. (2014) 'Not-So-Individual Voting: Patriarchal Control and Familial Hedging in Political Elections Around the World', *Journal of Women, Politics & Policy*, 35(4), pp. 349–78. https://doi.org/10.1080/1554477X.2014.955407.

Schwedler, J. (2015) *Jordan: The Quiescent Opposition*. Wilson Center. www.wilsoncenter.org/article/jordan-the-quiescent-opposition (accessed 30 July 2021).

Scott, J. C. (1972) 'Patron-Client Politics and Political Change in Southeast Asia', *American Political Science Review*, 66(1), pp. 91–113. https://doi.org/10.2307/1959280.

Selway, J. S. (2011) 'The Measurement of Cross-cutting Cleavages and Other Multidimensional Cleavage Structures', *Political Analysis*, 19(1), pp. 48–65.

Settles, I. H. and Buchanan, N. T. (2014) 'Multiple Groups, Multiple Identities, and Intersectionality', in Benet-Marinez, V. and Ying-yi, H. (eds.) *The Oxford Handbook of Multicultural Identity*. Oxford Library of Psychology. New York: Oxford University Press, pp. 160–80.

Singh, P. (2011) 'We-ness and Welfare: A Longitudinal Analysis of Social Development in Kerala, India', *World Development*, 39(2), pp. 282–93. https://doi.org/10.1016/j.worlddev.2009.11.025.

Singh, P. (2015) *How Solidarity Works for Welfare: Subnationalism and Social Development in India*. Cambridge Studies in Comparative Politics. New York: Cambridge University Press.

Singh, P. (2020) 'How Solidarity Is Controlling Contagion in Kerala', in *India in Transition*. Center for the Advanced Study of India. https://casi.sas.upenn .edu/iit/prernasingh (accessed 23 August 2022).

Skocpol, T. (1985) 'Bringing the State Back In: Strategies of Analysis in Current Research', in Evans, P. B., Rueschemeyer, D. and Skocpol, T. (eds.) *Bringing the State Back In*. Cambridge: Cambridge University Press, pp. 3–38. https://doi.org/10.1017/CBO9780511628283.002.

Smith, B. (2005) 'Life of the Party: The Origins of Regime Breakdown and Persistence under Single-Party Rule', *World Politics*, 57(3), pp. 421–51.

Sparks, R., Bottoms, A. E. and Hay, W. (1996) *Prisons and the Problem of Order*. Oxford: Clarendon Press.

Stokes, S. C. (2005) 'Perverse Accountability: A Formal Model of Machine Politics with Evidence from Argentina', *American Political Science Review*, 99(3), pp. 315–25. https://doi.org/10.1017/S0003055405051683.

Sunshine, J. and Tyler, T. R. (2003) 'The Role of Procedural Justice and Legitimacy in Shaping Public Support for Policing', *Law & Society Review*, 37(3), pp. 513–48.

Szwarcberg, M. (2012) 'Uncertainty, Political Clientelism, and Voter Turnout in Latin America: Why Parties Conduct Rallies in Argentina', *Comparative Politics*, 45(1), pp. 88–106.

Takane, T. (2008) 'Customary Land Tenure, Inheritance Rules, and Smallholder Farmers in Malawi', *Journal of Southern African Studies*, 34 (2), pp. 269–91.

Taylor, M. and Rae, D. (1969) 'An Analysis of Crosscutting between Political Cleavages', *Comparative Politics*, 1(4), pp. 534–47. https://doi.org/10.2307/421494.

Tetreault, M. A. (2014) 'Political Activism in Kuwait: Reform in Fits and Starts', in Lina Khatib and Ellen Lust (eds.) *Taking to the Streets: Activism and the Arab Uprisings*. Baltimore, MD: Johns Hopkins University Press, pp. 268–97.

Thachil, T. (2014) *Elite Parties, Poor Voters: How Social Services Win Votes in India*. New York: Cambridge University Press. https://doi.org/10.1017/CBO9781107707184.

The Carter Center (2012a) *Final Report of the Carter Center Mission to Witness the 2011–2012 Parliamentary Elections in Egypt*. Atlanta, GA: The Carter Center.

The Carter Center (2012b) *General National Congress Elections in Libya*. Atlanta, GA: The Carter Center.

Triandis, H. C. (1989) 'The Self and Social Behavior in Differing Cultural Contexts', *Psychological Review*, 96(3), pp. 506–20. https://doi.org/10.1037/0033-295X.96.3.506.

Triandis, H. C. (2001) 'Individualism-Collectivism and Personality', *Journal of Personality*, 69(6), pp. 907–24. https://doi.org/10.1111/1467-6494.696169.

Tsai, L. L. (2007) *Accountability without Democracy: Solidary Groups and Public Goods Provision in Rural China*. New York: Cambridge University Press. https://doi.org/10.1017/CBO9780511800115.

Turner, J. H. (1997) *The Institutional Order: Economy, Kinship, Religion, Polity, Law, and Education in Evolutionary and Comparative Perspective*. New York: Longman.

Tyler, T. R. (1990) *Justice, Self-interest, and the Legitimacy of Legal and Political Authority*. Chicago, IL: University of Chicago Press.

Tyler, T. R. (2006) *Why People Obey the Law*. Princeton, NJ: Princeton University Press.

UNDP and World Bank (2017) *(Re)building Core Government Functions in Fragile and Conflict Affected Settings: Joint Principles for Assessing Key Issues and Priorities*. UNDP and World Bank. www.undp.org/publications/rebuilding-core-government-functions-fragile-and-conflict-affected-settings.

Viskupic, F. and Wiltse, D. (2022) 'The Messenger Matters: Religious Leaders and Overcoming COVID-19 Vaccine Hesitancy', *PS: Political Science & Politics*, 55(3), 504–9. https://doi.org/10.1017/S104909652200004X.

Waring, T. M. (2011) 'Ethnic Forces in Collective Action: Diversity, Dominance, and Irrigation in Tamil Nadu', *Ecology and Society*, 16(4).

Waring, T. M. and Bell, A. V. (2013) 'Ethnic Dominance Damages Cooperation More than Ethnic Diversity: Results from Multi-ethnic Field Experiments in India', *Evolution and Human Behavior*, 34(6), pp. 398–404. https://doi.org/ 10.1016/j.evolhumbehav.2013.07.003.

Watkins, J. (2014) 'Seeking Justice: Tribal Dispute Resolution and Societal Transformation in Jordan', *International Journal of Middle East Studies*, 46 (1), pp. 31–49. https://doi.org/10.1017/S002074381300127X.

Watson, R. S. (1990) 'Corporate Property and Local Leadership in the Pearl River Delta, 1898–1941', in Esherick, J. W. and Rankin, M. B. (eds.) *Chinese Local Elites and Patterns of Dominance*. Berkeley: University of California Press, pp. 239–60.

Wedeen, L. (2002) 'Conceptualizing Culture: Possibilities for Political Science', *American Political Science Review*, 96(4), pp. 713–28.

Weir, S. (2007) *A Tribal Order: Politics and Law in the Mountains of Yemen*. London: British Museum Press.

Whaites, A. (2008) *States in Development: Understanding State-Building*. DFID Working Paper. London: Department for International Development. https://webarchive.nationalarchives.gov.uk/ukgwa/+/http://www.dfid.gov .uk/Documents/publications/State-in-Development-Wkg-Paper.pdf (accessed 23 August 2022).

Wiktorowicz, Q. (ed.) (2003) *Islamic Activism: A Social Movement Theory Approach*. Indiana Series in Middle East Studies. Bloomington: Indiana University Press.

van der Windt, P. and Voors, M. (2020) 'Traditional Leaders and the 2014–2015 Ebola Epidemic', *The Journal of Politics*, 82(4), pp 1607–11. https://doi.org/ 10.1086/708777.

World Bank (2017) *Why Secure Land Rights Matter*. World Bank. www.world bank.org/en/news/feature/2017/03/24/why-secure-land-rights-matter (accessed 18 May 2020).

World Values Survey (2018) World Value Survey Wave 6: Results by Country. World Values Survey. www.worldvaluessurvey.org/WVSDocumentationWV6 .jsp (accessed 18 July 2021).

Acknowledgements

I am grateful to Eman Aboud, Kate Baldwin, Melani Cammett, Janine Clark, Rabab El Mahdi, Karen E. Ferree, Prisca Jöst-Breneis, Adam S. Harris, Lauren Honig, Sarah Lockwood, Lauren MacLean, Stephen Ndegwa, Gibran Okar, Jeffrey Paller, Scott Radnitz, Isabell Schierenbeck, Ben Ross Schneider, Marwa Shalaby, David Waldner, participants at the Centre of Development Studies (Cambridge University) workshop, at the Workshop on Autocratic Politics and Populism (Hokkaido University), and two anonymous reviewers for constructive feedback on the manuscript; M. Stephan Okar for data analysis; Jennifer Bergman, Mina Ghassaban Kjellén, Gibran Okar, and Rose Shaber-Twedt for research and editorial assistance; and FORMAS (2016–00228, PI: Ellen Lust), the US National Science Foundation (1203343, PI: Ellen Lust), the Swedish Research Council (E0003801, PI: Pam Fredman; 2016–01687, PI: Ellen Lust), and Yale University for funding research and writing. Any remaining errors are, of course, my responsibility.

Cambridge Elements ☰

Politics of Development

Elements in the Series

A full series listing is available at: www.cambridge.org/EPOD

Lightning Source UK Ltd.
Milton Keynes UK
UKHW021444041222
413102UK00029B/528